SKINNY POTATOES

SKINNY POTATOES

by BARBARA GRUNES

Surrey Books

CHICAGO

SKINNY POTATOES is published by Surrey Books, Inc.,
230 E. Ohio St., Suite 120, Chicago, IL 60611.

First edition: 1 2 3 4 5

This book is manufactured in the United States of America.

Library of Congress Cataloging-in-Publication data:
Grunes, Barbara.
    Skinny potatoes / by Barbara Grunes. — 1st ed.
    190 p. cm. — (Skinny cookbooks series)
    Includes index.
    ISBN 0–940625–72–5 (cloth) $20.95
    ISBN 0–940625–69–5 (pbk.) $12.95
    1. Cookery (Potatoes) 2. Low-fat diet—Recipes. 3. Low-cholesterol
    diet—recipes. 4. Low-calorie diet—Recipes.
  I. Title. II. Series.
  TX803.P8G75 1993
  641.6'521—dc20

    93–19874
    CIP

Editorial and production: *Bookcrafters, Inc., Chicago*
Nutritional analyses: *Linda R. Yoakum, M.S., R.D.*
Art Director: *Hughes & Co., Chicago*
Cover and interior illustrations by *Laurel DiGangi*
Back cover photos courtesy The California Olive Industry and
  The National Live Stock and Meat Board

For free catalog and prices on quantity purchases, contact Surrey Books at the
address above.

This title is distributed to the trade by Publishers Group West.

Other titles in the "Skinny" Cookbooks Series:

Skinny Beef
Skinny Chocolate
Skinny Cookies, Cakes & Sweets
Skinny One-Pot Meals
Skinny Pastas

Skinny Pizzas
Skinny Seafood
Skinny Soups
Skinny Spices

Contents

1. Why "Skinny Potatoes"? 1

2. Appetizers and First Course Dishes 9

3. Soup 29

4. Stir-Fry Potatoes 45

5. Baked Potatoes with Toppings 61

6. Steamed Potatoes 103

7. Potato Salads 117

8. Potatoes on the Grill 129

9. Side Dishes 151

10. Breads and Desserts 167

    Index 179

Potato Nutrients Analysis
5 Oz. Cooked Portion

	Calories	Potassium (mg)	Fiber (gm)	Vit. C (mg)
White Potatoes				
Flesh only; baked, peeled afterward	132	554	3.4	18
Flesh only; boiled in skin, peeled afterward	123	537	2.1	18
Flesh only; boiled without skin, peeled before	122	465	1.6	10
Flesh and skin; baked	154	592	3.4	18
Microwaved, peeled after cooking	142	582	N.D.	21
Microwaved, with skin	149	643	N.D.	21
Potato skin only; baked	281	811	7.4	19
Sweet Potatoes				
Baked in skin, peeled afterward	145	494	4.2	35
Boiled without skin, mashed	149	261	4.2	24
Canned in syrup, drained solids only	154	273	N.D.	15

Note: Nutrients shown are those most affected by the cooking method or the presence of skin: potassium is water soluble so baking or boiling makes a difference; fiber comes primarily from the skin and outer portion of the potato; and vitamin C is affected by temperature and its duration.

1.
WHY "SKINNY POTATOES"?

T he "spud," "tater," "tatie," or "tato" is truly the vegetable that conquered the world, and it has fed and sustained millions of people for centuries.

The potato has been called "the peasant's staff of life" and "the gourmet's delight." The French term for the potato, *pomme de terre,* literally "apple of the earth," certainly rings with a more melodious sound than "spud."

Whatever it may be called or however described, the potato, with the exception of bread, is more popular and more frequently consumed by Americans than any other single food. Potato dishes regularly accompany breakfast, lunch, and dinner while the potato chip is probably America's favorite snack food. Virtually every American is well acquainted with the potato in its myriad cooked forms. This cookbook, however, will focus on "skinny potatoes," that is, low-fat, highly nutritious ways to prepare this universal food.

Skinny Potatoes takes this common tuber vegetable to new culinary heights. As a main ingredient in appetizers, salads, soups, breads, entrees, side dishes, stir-frys, grills, and even desserts, the potato is delicious, inexpensive, and healthful. We will use many varieties of potatoes in many ways: steamed, baked, boiled, or mashed, the versatile potato will be enhanced by many cooking techniques. By using non-stick pans and vegetable oil sprays, we will even fry potatoes without compromising their naturally healthful profile. And we will show you entirely new ways to employ potatoes, for instance using mashed potatoes as a great substitute for breadcrumbs in specialties such as crab cakes and stuffed peppers.

Some recipes in *Skinny Potatoes* include a touch of meat or poultry for flavor. For vegetarians and people watching their diets, however, potatoes can make a tasty meatless entree, high in vitamins and minerals and low in fat. Stir-fry potatoes, for example, form the basis of a simple but elegant one-dish meal.

Skinny Potatoes is a creative, good-for-you approach to an easy-to-cook, delightful-to-eat vegetable. For all their healthful qualities, potatoes are truly rich in fun and in flavor.

Ironically, potatoes have long been maligned by both chefs and home cooks. Chefs have often neglected the potato as an overly common and uninspiring side dish unworthy of gourmet cooking. Home cooks for decades wrongly perceived the potato as a highly caloric, non-nutritious, dumpy-looking, fattening vegetable.

However, in recent years, with the incredible surge in American awareness of and concern about health and nutrition, the potato has been redeemed. It is not the potato itself that is the calorie, fat, and sodium villain. It is how potato dishes have traditionally been prepared; what goes into them has caused the problem.

This book focuses upon the healthful properties of the potato and upon cooking methods, ingredients, and garnishes that retain the healthy and nutritious nature of the potato itself. The recipes in this book avoid ingredients that increase calories, cholesterol, fat content, and sodium, without sacrificing richness or flavor in these potato dishes.

In many cases we have used or recommended commercially available lower-fat or non-fat products. It is always preferable to use non-fat vegetable sprays, canola or olive oil, and the lowest-fat margarine in place of butter. The book strongly suggests egg substitutes, egg whites, low-fat mayonnaise, skim milk, non-fat yogurt, and low-fat cheeses in all potato dishes calling for such ingredients. As a salt substitute, we use light soy sauce, lemon juice, or a variety or interesting spices.

Spices and herbs are used in many of these recipes to complement or enhance flavor. It is just as easy to use spices and much healthier than piling on butter and salt—and you will lose nothing in taste. In fact, in most cases you will retain much more "potato" flavor. Deep-fat frying has been omitted altogether from the book.

While researching, creating, and then field-testing the recipes for this book, I became convinced that one could virtually "live" upon a diet of potatoes. While not advocating such a diet, I am truly convinced that you will increase your consumption of potatoes as you witness the delighted reactions of your family and guests to these recipes. You may rest assured that neither their health nor diet will be jeopardized but rather enhanced.

Also included in this book is a large chapter on baked potatoes, with a variety of toppings to make them complete meals. After all, baked potatoes are the most popular method of cooking potatoes.

A Brief History of the Potato

There is agreement among culinary historians that nomadic South American Indians collected wild potatoes on the central Andean plateau as early as six hundred B.C. These early wild potatoes grew at the incredible altitude of 12,000 to 14,000 feet in the vicinity of Lake Titicaca. Over centuries, the Indians developed potato agriculture, and potatoes were undoubtedly being cultivated as early as seven hundred fifty B.C. by the Incas in Peru, Ecuador, and northern Chile.

By the mid-16th century, when the Spanish conquistadors arrived, potatoes had become a staple of the great Inca civilization, which extended over thousands of miles in western South America. The potato was taken back to Spain by returning conquistadors. It was to be, ironically, a product from the New World with infinitely more value, in its own way, than the gold and silver the Europeans sought and plundered.

From Spain, the potato traveled eastward and northward into France, Germany, the Low Countries, and the Slavic lands. The potato made its first appearance in the British Isles in approximately 1586. Two conflicting accounts exist that may document this arrival. One, apparently the result of a misunderstanding, stems from an account written by John Gerand, a well-known 16th-century botanist, in his book *Herbal.* Gerand claimed that the potato came from Virginia, courtesy of Sir Francis Drake. However, what Gerand did not know was that Drake had taken the potatoes on board in Cartagena, Colombia, rather than in Virginia. Gerand gave some of the potatoes he had received from Drake to Sir Walter Raleigh, who planted them on his property in Ireland. So, regardless of their origin, the potatoes first planted in the British Isles certainly had an excellent pedigree, coming through two such notables as Drake and Raleigh.

The second account, somewhat of a legend in Ireland, suggests that the potato reached the Emerald Isle by accident when several Spanish ships accompanying the Spanish Armada foundered off the Irish coast. These ships were carrying Spanish-grown potatoes as part of their larder. The potatoes supposedly drifted to shore, and the Irish had their own prize of war.

Actually, the potato was relatively slow in gaining popularity in much of Europe, at least among some segments of the population. Superstitions and prejudices against the potato became abundant, and the potato soon became the most maligned vegetable in history. Some people refused to eat potatoes because they were not mentioned in the Bible. The potato was reviled by some clergy as being an unhealthy, erotic stimulant. During the later Renaissance, numerous ills, including leprosy, rickets, consumption, and warts, were blamed on the potato. Because the potato's nearest relatives were deadly nightshade and mandrake, both containing alkaloid poisons with hallucinogenic and narcotic effects, potatoes were shunned and sometimes even publicly burned to protect citizens from their addictive and potentially dangerous properties.

However, because of the potato's great adaptability to a wide range of growing conditions, its versatility, its high-yielding crops, and its high value as a nutrient, inevitably the superstitions and fears subsided and the potato assumed worldwide importance as a food crop.

Interestingly, a German cookbook published in 1581 contained a dozen potato recipes. By the early 18th century, potatoes had gained not only credibility but appeal. Frederick the Great of Prussia astutely saw the potato as a potential answer to periodic famine and ordered that potatoes be planted in his royal gardens and had his royal chefs devise new recipes for the potato. About the same time, King Louis XVI of France had potatoes planted in fields protected by royal guards in order to encourage their acceptance by the peasantry.

Potatoes played a crucial, but ultimately tragic, role in the lives of Irish peasants during the 19th century. Irish peasants had forestalled starvation for decades by consuming potatoes. When a devastating blight destroyed the potato crops in Ireland in 1845 and 1846, thousands died of starvation. This dubious episode in potato history did lend impetus, however, to one of history's greatest immigration surges to the United States.

Despite John Gerand's claim that the potato originated in North America, it is more likely that the potato was actually transferred back to America when Scotch-Irish immigrants settled in New England around 1719. The popularity of the potato spread throughout the Colonies, and it was soon a staple on the frontier, advancing across the country with the Western movement.

Yes, the humble potato has certainly had a teeter-totter history, but today its role is firmly established and its contribution to the dining satisfaction and good health of the world's people is anything but humble.

Varieties of Potatoes

There are eight species and literally thousands of varieties of potatoes. However, American consumers do not have nearly that much choice in purchasing potatoes, as only about 50 varieties are cultivated in the United States and only about 12 make up nearly 85 percent of the total United States' harvest. Also, to the frustration of many consumers, most American supermarkets do not identify potatoes by variety name, as is done in Europe, but tend to identify potatoes by where they were grown, for instance Maine or Idaho potatoes. Some markets sort and display potatoes by types: baking, all-purpose, boiling, new potatoes; or merely by color: white, yellow, red.

The following suggestions are ideas to limit the confusion and to help you find the particular variety of potato you require:

1. Consult the produce manager of your local supermarket. He may be able to identify potatoes by variety or obtain certain varieties for you.

2. Purchase potatoes from a produce market, an outdoor market, or a farmers' market and consult with the owners concerning the types of potatoes available.

3. Purchase your potatoes directly from a farmer or garden owner, who should know exactly which varieties of potatoes he or she has raised.

4. If you are lucky enough to have room for a garden, grow as many of the varieties you wish to use as your geographic region will permit.

Potatoes are also classified according to their starch content: high-starch, medium-starch, or low-starch. The starch content of a potato also indicates its moisture content, except in reverse proportion. High-starch potatoes are low in moisture while low-starch potatoes are high in moisture.

High-starch potatoes, which include russet or "baking" potatoes, are mealy textured and are excellent as baked potatoes.

Medium-starch potatoes are often called "all-purpose" potatoes. This includes such varieties as the Kennebec and the Superior. Medium-starch potatoes can be baked or mashed, but they will be slightly more watery than a standard baking potato. They are good for boiling, however, and hold their texture better in boiling water than high-starch varieties, which tend to crumble and become soggy.

Low-starch potatoes have a firm texture and are sometimes referred to as "waxy" because of the somewhat shiny appearance of the flesh. Low-starch varieties include most red potatoes, such as the Norland, Red Pontiac, and Red La Soda, as well as the Green Mountain. These varieties are moist and because they stay intact and hold their shape well, are best for boiling, steaming, grilling, roasting whole, and in dishes such as potato salad.

I might mention here that a "new potato" is not a separate variety of potato but simply one that is harvested before it reaches maturity. New potatoes are dug up in the spring and early summer, and they can often be purchased at farmers' markets or at produce stands. Many people grow potatoes in home gardens just so they can have new potatoes in the spring. Unlike mature potatoes, which will keep for several weeks, new potatoes can be held only a few days. New potatoes are low in starch and are firm and moist. They are absolutely wonderful steamed or boiled.

Selecting Potatoes for Purchase

While there are four potato harvests in the United States, more than 75 percent of all potatoes consumed in this country are harvested during the fall months. Look for potatoes that are firm, smooth-surfaced, well-shaped, and heavy in the hand. Avoid potatoes that have sprouted or potatoes with cracks, withered or wrinkled skins, or discolorations such as green or dark areas. Potatoes that have many "eyes," bumps, or indentations are not necessarily "bad"; but there is greater waste when peeled. Do not be overly concerned about the size of potatoes; it is better to look at the quality than the size.

A word about green-skinned potatoes. The greenish tinge to the skin indicates the possible presence of solanine, a chemical compound that can make you sick if you eat it in large amounts. Solanine is neutralized by the cooking process, but I recommend avoiding green-skinned potatoes or peeling them before use.

When shopping for sweet potatoes, select small or medium-sized specimens, as they are the most tender. Use the same criteria as in selecting white potatoes: firm, heavy, well-shaped, and without bruises, cuts, or cracks. To avoid peeling headaches, do not buy sweet potatoes with strange twists or knobs. Generally, the darker the skin of a sweet potato, the sweeter and moister it will be.

Storing Potatoes

If you purchase potatoes in a plastic bag, remove them at home. If you want to store them in a container, the best type is a net bag. Do not wash potatoes before storage.

Potatoes should be stored in a cool (40°–50° F.), well-ventilated place with good air circulation. Ideally, potatoes should be purchased in small enough quantities so that they can be used within two weeks. However, potatoes that are properly stored can last throughout a winter. If long-term storage is desired, it is a good idea to separate potatoes individually or to layer them with newspapers so that if one turns bad, it will not spoil the lot.

Try to avoid storing potatoes in your refrigerator, although they will hold there for a short time if they stay dry.

Store sweet potatoes as you would white potatoes, in a cool, dry, well-ventilated area. Like white potatoes, sweet potatoes should last at least two weeks.

Before cooking, scrub potatoes thoroughly. Remove eyes and cut out any soft or discolored spots, greenish-tinted skin, or other blemishes. If you are peeling potatoes, use a vegetable peeler or paring knife, trying to remove as little flesh as possible.

The Nutritional Powerhouse

Carbohydrates such as the no-fat, complex carbohydrates of potatoes are a treasure trove of essential nutrients. And if you eat the skin, you get the bonus of added fiber. A medium-sized baked potato (7 ounces) is a nutritional bargain at about 200 calories. It provides almost one-half of your daily need for vitamin C, about as much potassium as a banana, almost 5 grams of protein, a variety of vitamins and minerals, and it is cholesterol free and low in sodium. One-half of a boiled potato has only about 67 calories, but hold the butter, sour cream, and other fat-laden toppings.

Baked sweet potatoes have about the same calories and slightly less protein than white potatoes, but they contain more calcium and vitamin C. Even more important, they are an excellent source of vitamin A. A half-cup of baked sweet potato has over 2,000 retinol equivalents of vitamin A, more than twice the recommended daily intake for men and almost three times the recommendation for women.

My good friend Mary Abbot Hess, a registered dietitian and past president of the American Dietetic Association, wants you to know that "in addition, beta-carotene, the pigment that gives sweet potatoes their orange color, is an antioxidant, which may help protect against cancer and heart disease." She says, "What could be better: *Skinny Potatoes* recipes taste great while promoting health and protecting against disease."

Finally, I would like to encourage the use of leftover potatoes, where they can be successfully employed in a recipe. However, the pejorative, "cold potato," often applied to an unresponsive or dull person, has its origin in the traditional lack of zest and flavor in leftover spuds. Most recipes and dishes will benefit by the use of freshly cooked potatoes.

In Closing

Jean Brillat-Savarin, the author of a celebrated 18th-century work on gastronomy, *The Physiology of Taste,* said of the potato: "None for me. I appreciate the potato only as a protection against famine; except for that, I know of nothing more eminently tasteless." What a shame that Brillat-Savarin did not possess a copy of *Skinny Potatoes.*

2.
APPETIZERS AND FIRST COURSE DISHES

Potato Crab Cakes

Salsa-Stuffed New Potatoes

Potato-Stuffed Red Peppers

Catonese-Fried Stuffed Peppers

Potato Spinach Balls

Potato Vegetable Kabobs

Potato Wedges with Italian Tuna Sauce

Potato Pancakes with Ginger Yogurt

Potato-Zucchini Pancakes with Indian Sauce

Potato Pâté with Mushroom Sauce

Russian Potato-Cheese Dumplings

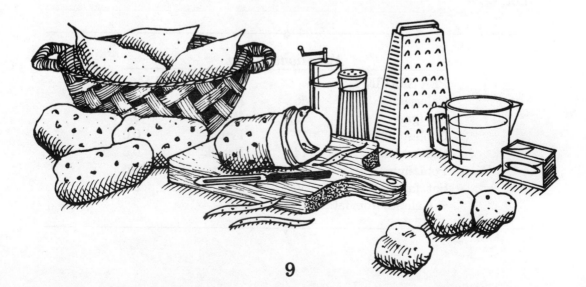

POTATO CRAB CAKES

Potato Crab Cakes are really crab-flavored potato pancakes. They can be prepared in advance, just reheat for serving time. Surimi, or imitation crab, is available at the fish counter of most supermarkets. It is made using a Japanese process in which fish is processed, flavored, and re-formed into a crab-like shape. It is then cooked. Most of the fish used is pollack. Some real crab is also included. This product is high in protein and lower in cholesterol and fat than some fish. It does contain some sugar and salt.

8 Servings

2 cups plain cooked mashed potatoes
1 cup crabmeat, or surimi (imitation crabmeat)
2 egg whites, slightly beaten
½ teaspoon Worcestershire sauce
¼ teaspoon red pepper flakes
¼ cup parsley, minced
   Olive oil, or non-stick cooking spray
2 teaspoons margarine

 eel, cook, mash, and cool potatoes. Spoon potatoes into a mixing bowl. Mix in crabmeat, egg whites, Worcestershire sauce, red pepper flakes, and parsley.

Shape batter into patties and set on a plate. Spray a non-stick frying pan with oil and add margarine. Melt margarine over medium heat. Fry Potato Crab Cakes about 2 minutes on each side or until cakes have browned and are cooked. Remove to individual plates and serve hot.

Nutritional Data

PER SERVING		EXCHANGES	
Calories:	56	Milk:	0.0
Fat (gm):	0.9	Veg.:	0.0
Cholesterol (mg):	17	Fruit:	0.0
Sodium (mg):	114	Bread:	0.5
Potassium (mg):	173	Meat:	0.5
Sat. fat (gm):	0.2	Fat:	0.0
% Calories from fat:	15		

Salsa-Stuffed New Potatoes

Small cooked new potatoes are really good to eat just as they are, but if you scoop out the center and add spicy salsa, you have a nutritious, delicious, very special appetizer.

8 Servings

16 small new potatoes, skin on

Spicy Salsa

2 medium tomatoes, peeled, seeded, chopped

2 jalapeño peppers, seeded (it is always a good idea to use rubber gloves when handling hot peppers)

½ cup cilantro, chopped

1 tablespoon black pitted olives, chopped

1 teaspoon lime juice, fresh-squeezed

⅛ teaspoon cayenne pepper

¼ teaspoon ground cumin

 crub potatoes. Cook, covered, with water over medium-high heat until just fork tender, about 15 to 20 minutes. Drain potatoes; cool. Trim bottom of potatoes so they will stand on serving plate without rolling. Slice potatoes in halves, and scoop out meat, using a melon scoop or teaspoon; reserve for another meal or discard. Leave a thin layer of potato attached to the skin. Place potatoes on serving dish.

Spicy Salsa: Prepare while potatoes are cooking. To make salsa, toss together tomatoes, peppers, cilantro, olives, lime juice, cayenne, and cumin. Spoon salsa into cavity of each potato. Serve hot. You might wish to put extra salsa in a small bowl and pass it with potatoes for those wanting an extra helping. A side dish of plain non-fat yogurt might also look good on the serving tray for those who want to fill extra potato skins with yogurt.

Nutritional Data

PER SERVING		EXCHANGES	
Calories:	108	Milk:	0.0
Fat (gm):	0.4	Veg.:	1.0
Cholesterol (mg):	0	Fruit:	0.0
Sodium (mg):	45	Bread:	1.0
Potassium (mg):	523	Meat:	0.0
Sat. fat (gm):	0.1	Fat:	0.0
% Calories from fat:	3		

POTATO-STUFFED RED PEPPERS

The classic stuffed pepper is a glory of Hungarian cuisine. We have lightened the recipe, using a tasty potato stuffing instead of ground meat or lamb. Since this recipe is an appetizer, use small red bell peppers. You can prepare potatoes the day before or use leftover plain mashed potatoes.

8 Servings

Potato Stuffing

Olive oil, or non-stick cooking spray
- ½ cup red onions, chopped
- 3 cloves garlic, minced
- 1 cup celery, sliced
- 3 red potatoes, about 1½ lbs., peeled, cooked, mashed, cooled
- ½ teaspoon each ingredient: cayenne pepper, oregano

- 8 small red bell peppers

Red Pepper Sauce

Olive oil, or non-stick cooking spray
- 2 medium-large red bell peppers, seeded, chopped
- 3 shallots, minced
- 1½ cups plain non-fat yogurt
- ¼ teaspoon oregano

Potato Stuffing: Spray a non-stick frying pan and cook onions, garlic, and celery, covered, over medium heat, stirring occasionally. Stir in mashed potatoes. Season with cayenne and oregano. Set aside.

With a small sharp knife, cut a ½-inch circle around stem end of each pepper. Remove lid and seeds. Wash pepper and drain; dry on paper towel. Using a spoon, stuff peppers with potato mixture.

Place peppers in 9 × 13-inch baking pan. Pour ½ cup water into pan. Preheat oven to 375° F. Bake peppers 20 minutes or until hot and cooked.

Red Pepper Sauce: Prepare while peppers are cooking. Spray a non-stick frying pan and saute peppers and shallots until peppers are tender, about 5 to 6 minutes, stirring occasionally. Cool and puree. Pour pureed mixture into small bowl. Mix in yogurt and oregano. Taste to adjust seasonings.

When ready to serve, spoon a pool of sauce onto each each dish. Using a sloted spoon, set a stuffed pepper in center of sauce. Serve hot.

Nutritional Data

PER SERVING		EXCHANGES	
Calories:	138	Milk:	0.5
Fat (gm):	0.5	Veg.:	1.5
Cholesterol (mg):	11	Fruit:	0.0
Sodium (mg):	63	Bread:	1.0
Potassium (mg):	632	Meat:	0.0
Sat. fat (gm):	0.1	Fat:	0.0
% Calories from fat:	3		

CANTONESE-FRIED STUFFED PEPPERS

◆

This recipe can easily be prepared ahead of time and reheated for company or when ready to serve.

◆

12 Servings

- 2 cups plain cooked mashed potatoes
- ¼ cup water chestnuts, minced
- 4 green onions, minced
- ¼ cup bean sprouts, washed, drained
- ½ teaspoon ginger root, fresh-grated
- ¼ teaspoon garlic powder
- 3 green or red bell peppers, cut into quarters
  Canola oil, or non-stick cooking spray
- 2 tablespoons cornstarch
- 2 teaspoons light soy sauce
- 1 teaspoon sugar
- ½ cup water

S poon potatoes into deep mixing bowl. Blend in water chestnuts, onions, bean sprouts, ginger, and garlic.

Using a spoon, stuff pepper wedges with potatoes. Spray a large non-stick frying pan and cook stuffed pepper wedges, positioning them stuffing side down, over medium heat. Do not turn peppers over. Cook 2 minutes.

Mix cornstarch, soy sauce, sugar, and water in a glass. Add to frying pan. Cover pan immediately and continue cooking about 8 minutes. Using a spatula, carefully invert peppers onto serving dish. Serve wedges, potato side up. Stuffed peppers will be crusty on top.

◆

Nutritional Data

PER SERVING		EXCHANGES	
Calories:	51	Milk:	0.0
Fat (gm):	0.3	Veg.:	1.0
Cholesterol (mg):	1	Fruit:	0.0
Sodium (mg):	140	Bread:	0.5
Potassium (mg):	168	Meat:	0.0
Sat. fat (gm):	0.1	Fat:	0.0
% Calories from fat:	2		

POTATO SPINACH BALLS

Potato Spinach Balls are good as an appetizer. Serve with cut crisp vegetables and perhaps a salsa for dipping. An alternative is to use these vegetarian potato balls with spaghetti or other pasta as a main dish.

---

8 Servings

- 1 package frozen chopped spinach, 10 ozs., defrosted, drained
- 3 cups plain cooked mashed potatoes
- 2 egg whites, slightly beaten
- 4 cloves garlic, minced
- ½ cup parsley, minced
- ½ teaspoon each ingredient: ground mace, marjoram

  Olive oil, or non-stick cooking spray
- 2 tablespoons, or to taste, Parmesan cheese, fresh-grated

  Toothpicks

 o prepare potato balls, squeeze spinach dry and place in deep mixing bowl. Mix in mashed potatoes, egg whites, garlic, parsley, mace, and marjoram. Using wet hands, shape mixture into 1½-inch balls; place on tray or plate.

Spray a non-stick frying pan and fry potato balls until cooked crisp and golden brown. Remove to serving plate, sprinkle with Parmesan cheese, and surround with cut vegetables. Serve hot and provide toothpicks.

Nutritional Data

PER SERVING		EXCHANGES	
Calories:	86	Milk:	0.0
Fat (gm):	1.0	Veg.:	0.5
Cholesterol (mg):	3	Fruit:	0.0
Sodium (mg):	314	Bread:	1.0
Potassium (mg):	382	Meat:	0.0
Sat. fat (gm):	0.6	Fat:	0.0
% Calories from fat:	10		

POTATO VEGETABLE KABOBS

Double-pronged skewers are just what the name implies, a skewer fitted with two prongs. This makes it possible to kabob small items of food such as potatoes, peppers, and tomato wedges without having them slip around the skewer. Double-pronged skewers are available at gourmet shops and from Gamatech, PO Box 8069, Santa Rosa, California 95155; phone 1–408–291–5220.
These kabobs make a festive first course to a grilled meal. For a change, you might serve the vegetables on a platter and ask your guests to make their own kabobs. Everyone likes to participate in the cooking process.

4 Servings

- 8 new potatoes, skin on, scrubbed
- 1 large red or green bell pepper, seeded, cut into 1½-in. pieces
- 1 medium red onion, sliced
- 1 medium zucchini, cut into ½-in. pieces
- 4 small pickled peppers, or sport peppers, drained
- ¼ cup balsamic vinegar
- ½ teaspoon each ingredient: oregano, basil
- ¼ teaspoon black pepper, fresh-ground

 Scrub potatoes. Place potatoes in saucepan and cover with water; bring to a boil over medium-high heat. Reduce heat to medium and continue cooking until potatoes are fork tender, about 15 to 20 minutes. Drain; pat dry. Cool and cut in half.

Thread skewers with peppers, onions, zucchini, potatoes, and pickled peppers.

In a small bowl, mix vinegar, oregano, basil, and black pepper. Brush kabobs with vinegar mixture.

Grill kabobs over hot coals on greased grill screen or rack, about 6 inches from heat, rotating kabobs every 1 to 2 minutes until done to taste. Remove kabobs to individual dishes and serve hot. Allow guests to remove the vegetables from the kabobs themselves.

Nutritional Data

PER SERVING		EXCHANGES	
Calories:	136	Milk:	0.0
Fat (gm):	0.3	Veg.:	1.0
Cholesterol (mg):	0	Fruit:	0.0
Sodium (mg):	134	Bread:	1.5
Potassium (mg):	601	Meat:	0.0
Sat. fat (gm):	0	Fat:	0.0
% Calories from fat:	2		

POTATO WEDGES WITH ITALIAN TUNA SAUCE

Crisp potato wedges are made by cutting and baking potatoes into horizontal wedges, seasoning and baking them. Make extra potatoes, as they go fast.

8 Servings

Olive oil, or non-stick cooking spray

4 large baking potatoes, about 2 lbs., skin on, scrubbed, each cut into 6 horizontal wedges

2 tablespoon Canola oil for brushing potatoes, option.:

1 teaspoon each ingredient: garlic powder, oregano, basil

¼ teaspoon black pepper, fresh-ground

Italian Tuna Sauce

1 can water packed tuna, 6½ ozs., drained

⅓ cup cholesterol-free, reduced-calorie mayonnaise

1 anchovy filet, drained, washed, patted dry, cut into small pieces

1 teaspoon capers

1½ tablespoons lemon juice, fresh-squeezed

⅛ teaspoon black pepper, fresh-ground

 reheat oven to 400° F. Spray a non-stick baking sheet and set aside.

Brush potato wedges lightly with oil, optional. Arrange potatoes on prepared baking sheet. Sprinkle with garlic, oregano, basil and pepper. Set potatoes on middle rack of oven, and bake 45 to 50 minutes or until tender on the inside, crusty and golden brown on the outside. Turn potatoes 3 or 4 times during cooking so that all sides are browned.

Remove potatoes to serving dish and arrange in a circle around tuna sauce. Serve while potatoes are hot.

Italian Tuna Sauce: Prepare while potatoes are baking. Using food processor fitted with steel blade, puree tuna, mayonnaise, anchovy filet, capers, lemon juice, and pepper. If sauce seems too thick, thin with vegetable stock or dry white wine.

Nutritional Data

PER SERVING		EXCHANGES	
Calories:	132	Milk:	0.0
Fat (gm):	3.0	Veg.:	0.0
Cholesterol (mg):	8	Fruit:	0.0
Sodium (mg):	123	Bread:	1.0
Potassium (mg):	386	Meat:	1.0
Sat. fat (gm):	0.1	Fat:	0.0
% Calories from fat:	20		

POTATO PANCAKES WITH GINGER YOGURT

Remember to allow the batter to stand 20 minutes before making the pancakes.

8 Servings

Pancake Batter

- 4 large baking potatoes, about 2 lbs., peeled
- ¾ cup onions, grated
- 2 egg whites, slightly beaten
- ¼ teaspoon baking soda
- ½ teaspoon basil
- Canola oil, or non-stick cooking spray

Ginger Yogurt

- 2 cups plain non-fat yogurt
- 2 teaspoons candied ginger, minced
- ½ cup chives, minced

Pancake Batter: Grate potatoes into deep mixing bowl, working quickly as potatoes brown fast. Mix in remaining batter ingredients except the oil. Cover bowl with plastic wrap and let stand at room temperature or in refrigerator 20 minutes. Stir before using.

Ginger Yogurt: In separate bowl mix together yogurt, ginger, and chives. Cover and refrigerate; stir before serving.

Spray a large non-stick frying pan, or use Canola oil. Pour batter onto hot pan by the tablespoon, making silver-dollar-size pancakes, about 1½ to 2 inches in diameter. Fry pancakes on both sides until cooked and golden brown. Turn once.

Place bowl of ginger yogurt on serving plate and surround with hot pancakes. Serve with toothpicks and cocktail napkins.

Nutritional Data

PER SERVING		EXCHANGES	
Calories:	115	Milk:	0.5
Fat (gm):	0.2	Veg.:	0.0
Cholesterol (mg):	1	Fruit:	0.0
Sodium (mg):	87	Bread:	1.0
Potassium (mg):	495	Meat:	0.0
Sat. fat (gm):	0.1	Fat:	0.0
% Calories from fat:	2		

Potato-Zucchini Pancakes with Indian Sauce

The yogurt-based, Indian-flavored sauce makes these silver-dollar-size pancakes a treat as an appetizer or first course. You can also make the pancakes larger and serve them as a main dish or side dish.

8 Servings

Indian Yogurt Sauce

- 1 cup plain non-fat yogurt
- ½ teaspoon garlic powder
- ½ cup tomato, seeded, chopped
- 2 tablespoons cilantro, minced
- Drops of hot red sauce, to taste

Pancake Batter

- 3 large baking potatoes, about 1½ lbs., peeled
- 1 cup zucchini, grated
- 2 egg whites
- ¼ teaspoon each ingredient: white pepper, cumin
- 2 tablespoons all-purpose flour
- ½ teaspoon baking powder
- ¼ cup dried onion flakes
- Olive oil, or non-stick cooking spray

Indian Yogurt Sauce: In a small bowl, mix together yogurt, garlic powder, tomato, cilantro, and hot red sauce. Cover lightly and refrigerate until serving time. Stir sauce before serving.

Pancake Batter: Working quickly as potatoes brown fast, grate potatoes into deep mixing bowl. Mix in zucchini, egg whites, pepper, cumin, flour, baking powder, and dried onion flakes. Cover bowl with plastic wrap and let stand at room temperature or in refrigerator 20 minutes. Stir before using.

Spray a large non-stick frying pan, or use oil. Pour batter onto hot frying pan by the tablespoon, making 2-inch pancakes. Fry pancakes on both sides until cooked and golden brown. Turn once.

Position pancakes on serving dish with bowl of sauce. Serve hot with toothpicks and cocktail napkins.

Nutritional Data

PER SERVING		EXCHANGES	
Calories:	95	Milk:	0.0
Fat (gm):	0.2	Veg.:	0.0
Cholesterol (mg):	0	Fruit:	0.0
Sodium (mg):	62	Bread:	1.0
Potassium (mg):	432	Meat:	0.5
Sat. fat (gm):	0.1	Fat:	0.0
% Calories from fat:	2		

POTATO PÂTÉ WITH MUSHROOM SAUCE

This flavorful potato pâté with a colorful middle layer of carrots is very pretty when sliced.

---

12 Servings

Potato Pâté

Margarine to brush pan

4 large boiling potatoes, about 2 lbs., scrubbed, peeled, cooked, mashed, cooled

½ cup egg substitute

¼ cup skim milk

2 teaspoons each ingredient: cornstarch, minced parsley

½ teaspoon oregano

1½ cups cooked carrots, pureed

1 egg white, slightly beaten

¼ teaspoon each ingredient: salt, white pepper

Mushroom Sauce

Olive oil, or non-stick cooking spray

1 lb. white mushrooms, cleaned, chopped

3 shallots, minced

¼ cup low-salt Chicken Stock (see Index)

¼ teaspoon black pepper, fresh-ground

1½ cups plain non-fat yogurt

Potato Pâté: Brush a 6-cup loaf pan with margarine. Preheat oven to 350° F.

In large mixing bowl, beat potatoes with egg substitute, milk, cornstarch, parsley, and oregano. Divide potato mixture in half and gently pack one-half into bottom of prepared loaf pan.

Place carrots in bowl and mix in egg white, salt, and pepper. Spread carrot mixture over potatoes. Gently layer remaining potato mixture over carrot mixture. Cover pan with aluminum foil.

Set a pan larger and deeper than the loaf pan in oven. Place loaf pan in center of larger pan. Pour hot water into larger pan until water is about 1 inch from top of loaf pan.

Bake pâté 55 minutes to 1 hour. When done, a bamboo skewer inserted into pâté will come out dry. Cool pâté in oven, with door open, 10 minutes.

Mushroom Sauce: Prepare while pâté is baking. Spray or oil a non-stick frying pan. Saute mushrooms, shallots, and chicken stock over medium heat, stirring occasionally until mushrooms are cooked and tender. Season with pepper. Puree cooled mushrooms and spoon them into a bowl. Mix in yogurt. Cool to room temperature.

To serve, loosen pâté by running a sharp knife around edges of pan. Invert pâté onto serving dish. Spoon a pool of sauce into center or each plate. Slice pâté with sharp knife and place a slice in center of sauce.

Nutritional Data

PER SERVING		EXCHANGES	
Calories:	92	Milk:	0.0
Fat (gm):	0.7	Veg.:	0.0
Cholesterol (mg):	1	Fruit:	0.0
Sodium (mg):	115	Bread:	1.0
Potassium (mg):	500	Meat:	1.0
Sat. fat (gm):	0.1	Fat:	0.0
% Calories from fat:	6		

RUSSIAN POTATO-CHEESE DUMPLINGS

Pierogi are Russian and Polish dumplings. They make an excellent appetizer, side dish, or even dessert.

8 Servings

Pastry

- 2 cups all-purpose flour
- 2 egg whites, slightly beaten
- ½ cup water

Potato-Cheese Filling

- 2 teaspoons margarine
- ¼ cup green onions, minced
- 1½ cups plain cooked mashed potatoes, hot
- 3¼ ozs. skim ricotta cheese
- ¼ teaspoon nutmeg, grated

Pastry: In a mixing bowl, combine flour, egg whites, and water. Knead until a soft dough is formed. Shape into dough ball, and cover bowl with plastic wrap to keep dough moist.

Potato-Cheese Filling: Melt margarine in non-stick frying pan over medium heat. Saute onions 3 minutes, stirring occasionally. In small separate bowl, mix mashed potatoes with cheese; add mixture to frying pan and stir. Sprinkle with nutmeg and blend all ingredients together.

To assemble dumplings, roll out to ¼-inch thickness half of dough on lightly floured pastry cloth. Cut out 2½- or 3-inch circles with cookie cutter. Mound 1 teaspoon of filling in center of each cut out; then fold dough in half to form a crescent shape. Squeeze edges together, crimping dough securely. Continue until all dumplings have been prepared.

Bring a large pot of water to boil over medium-high heat. Add 12 dumplings. Cover and cook until dumplings float to surface, 4 to 5 minutes. Using a slotted spoon, remove dumplings to greased tray or plate. Continue until all dumplings have been prepared.

Serve dumplings hot. You may want to serve them with plain non-fat yogurt mixed with snipped chives.

Nutritional Data

PER SERVING		EXCHANGES	
Calories:	169	Milk:	0.0
Fat (gm):	1.9	Veg.:	0.0
Cholesterol (mg):	4	Fruit:	0.0
Sodium (mg):	159	Bread:	2.0
Potassium (mg):	184	Meat:	0.5
Sat. fat (gm):	0.8	Fat:	0.0
% Calories from fat:	10		

3.
SOUP

Low-Salt Chicken Stock

Low-Salt Vegetable Stock

Potato-Mussel Saffron Soup

Vichyssoise

New York City Clam Chowder

Maine Clam Chowder

Potato Fish Chowder

Potato Curry Soup

Summer Potato Buttermilk Soup

Beet Soup with Potatoes and Yogurt

Potato Pistou

Goulash Soup

Potato Barley Soup

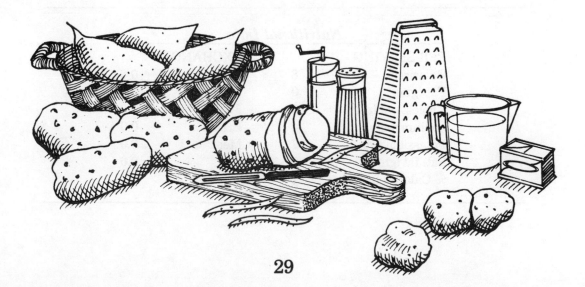

LOW-SALT CHICKEN STOCK

Save uncooked chicken bones in a plastic bag in the freezer for making chicken stock.

7 Servings (1 cup each)

1   lb. chicken breasts, skin discarded, leave
    bones intact
    Chicken bones, uncooked, from 4 chicken
       breasts, discard visible fat
2   onions, sliced
3   stalks celery, sliced
3   carrots, sliced
½   cup parsley sprigs
1   parsley root, sliced
1   large boiling potato, about ½ lb., peeled, sliced
½   teaspoon pepper

D iscard any fat found on chicken or bones. Place chicken and bones in soup pot or other large pan. Add remaining ingredients; cover with 3½ quarts water. Bring soup to a boil, reduce heat to simmer, and continue cooking about 1½ hours or until done. Skim off any foam that rises to surface. Cool soup.

   Remove chicken, bones, and vegetables. Strain cooled soup through a double layer of cheesecloth. Skim off fat. Place soup stock in covered container and refrigerate or freeze until needed.

Nutritional Data

PER SERVING		EXCHANGES	
Calories:	8	Milk:	0.0
Fat (gm):	0	Veg.:	0.0
Cholesterol (mg):	0	Fruit:	0.0
Sodium (mg):	4	Bread:	0.0
Potassium (mg):	27	Meat:	0.0
Sat. fat (gm):	0	Fat:	0.0
% Calories from fat:	1		

LOW-SALT VEGETABLE STOCK

This is a slimmed down version of basic vegetable stock and can be used as a base in many soups and dishes in this book. To store stock, pour cooked soup into ice cube tray and freeze. Dislodge the frozen cubes and store in a plastic bag in the freezer until needed.

12 Servings (¾ cup each)

Canola oil, or non-stick cooking spray
4 cloves garlic, crushed
2 cups onions, roughly chopped
3 ribs celery, sliced
3 cups carrots, peeled, sliced
1 cup turnip, sliced
1 cup boiling potato, peeled, cubed
½ cup parsley, chopped
2 bay leaves
½ teaspoon each ingredient: thyme, pepper

pray soup pot, or coat with oil. Saute garlic, onions, and celery 5 minutes, covered, over medium heat, stirring occasionally. Add remaining ingredients and continue cooking 5 minutes. Add 3 quarts water. Bring stock to boil; reduce heat to simmer. Continue cooking 1¾ hours or until done. Stir stock occasionally.

When soup is cool, strain through double layer of cheesecloth. Use remaining vegetables as a side dish or in a stew. Store cooled stock in refrigerator or freezer.

Nutritional Data

PER SERVING		EXCHANGES	
Calories:	4	Milk:	0.0
Fat (gm):	0	Veg.:	0.0
Cholesterol (mg):	0	Fruit:	0.0
Sodium (mg):	3	Bread:	0.0
Potassium (mg):	23	Meat:	0.0
Sat. fat (gm):	0	Fat:	0.0
% Calories from fat:	3		

POTATO-MUSSEL SAFFRON SOUP

What a good soup for a complete meal in a bowl. Remember, do not use mussels that have opened before cooking or do not open after cooking. Garnish with chopped chives or green onions.

8 Servings

    Olive oil, or non-stick cooking spray
- 6 shallots, minced
- 3 cloves garlic
- 3 large boiling potatoes, about 1½ lbs., peeled, diced
- 3 large carrots, sliced thin
- 2 leeks, cleaned under cold running water, sliced, white part only
- 32 mussels, washed, debearded
- 4 ripe tomatoes, peeled, seeded, chopped
- 1 can, 16 ozs., crushed tomatoes
- ½ cup parsley, chopped
- 2 bay leaves
- 1 teaspoon fennel seeds
- ¼ teaspoon each ingredient: saffron, soaked in 1 tablespoon water, white pepper

Spray or oil a large saucepan or soup pot and saute shallots, garlic, potatoes, carrots, and leeks, covered, over medium heat 5 minutes. Add 1 quart water and bring to boil. Add remaining ingredients except mussels. Reduce heat to medium and continue cooking 10 to 15 minutes or until vegetables are tender. Add mussels, cover, and cook 3 to 5 minutes or until mussels are done.

    Discard any unopened mussels and discard bay leaves. Taste to adjust seasonings. Serve hot.

Nutritional Data

PER SERVING		EXCHANGES	
Calories:	140	Milk:	0.0
Fat (gm):	1.4	Veg.:	3.0
Cholesterol (mg):	21	Fruit:	0.0
Sodium (mg):	359	Bread:	0.5
Potassium (mg):	0	Meat:	0.5
Sat. fat (gm):	0.1	Fat:	0.0
% Calories from fat:	9		

VICHYSSOISE

Vichyssoise is one of the most popular of all potato-based soups, good served hot or cold. Leeks are very sandy, so wash them well under cold running water.

8 Servings

Canola oil, or non-stick cooking spray
4 cups leeks, sliced, use white part only
1 cup white onions, sliced
4 large boiling potatoes, about 2 lbs., peeled, sliced thin
5 cups low-salt Chicken Stock (see Index)
1 can, 13 ozs., evaporated skim milk
½ teaspoon white pepper
¼ teaspoon salt
2 tablespoons fresh mint, chopped
½ cup plain non-fat yogurt

Spray soup pot or other large pan or coat lightly with oil. Saute leeks, onions, and potatoes, covered, about 10 minutes over medium heat. Stir vegetables occasionally.

Add chicken stock. Simmer 15 minutes. Stir in milk. Again cover and simmer soup another 10 minutes. Stir occasionally.

Cool soup and puree. Return pureed soup to clean pot and stir in pepper, salt, mint, and yogurt. Simmer soup until hot but do not bring to boil. Ladle into bowls and sprinkle with mint. Vichyssoise is good hot or cold.

Nutritional Data

PER SERVING		EXCHANGES	
Calories:	168	Milk:	0.5
Fat (gm):	0.5	Veg.:	2.0
Cholesterol (mg):	2	Fruit:	0.0
Sodium (mg):	150	Bread:	1.0
Potassium (mg):	650	Meat:	0.0
Sat. fat (gm):	0.1	Fat:	0.0
% Calories from fat:	3		

NEW YORK CITY CLAM CHOWDER

Chowder from Manhattan is similar to that from New England only in that both contain clams. The New York variety is really a tomato-based vegetable soup with clams. Remember that clams that are open before cooking and those that are unopened after cooking should be discarded.

Historically the word "chowder" is from the French "chaudiere," which means cauldron or large pot. Many French cooked in such large containers when they came to North America.

8 Servings

32 Littleneck clams, or other fresh small clams, washed well
   Olive oil, or non-stick cooking spray
4 all-purpose potatoes, about 2 lbs., scrubbed, peeled, cubed or sliced
1 cup onions, sliced
2 carrots
1 can, 28 ozs. crushed tomatoes, include juice
½ cup clam juice
⅓ cup parsley, chopped
½ teaspoon thyme
¼ teaspoon pepper
2 bay leaves
¼ teaspoon hot red sauce, optional

 ash clams and discard any that are open. Put clams in large saucepan; add 3 cups water. Cover and cook over medium-high heat 5 minutes or until clams open. Discard any clams that do not open. Leave clams in shells. Strain liquid through double layer of cheesecloth and reserve for chowder.

Spray large pot or coat lightly with oil. Saute potatoes, onions, and carrots about 5 minutes, covered, over medium heat, stirring occasionally. Mix in crushed tomatoes, clam juice, parsley, thyme, pepper, bay leaves, and hot red sauce. Add strained clam juice.

Bring chowder to boil. Reduce heat to simmer; cover. Cook 45 minutes or until all vegetables are tender. Add clams in shells. Cook another 3 minutes. Discard bay leaves.

Ladle chowder into deep bowls. Put a bowl for discarded clam shells on table. Serve chowder hot.

Nutritional Data

PER SERVING		EXCHANGES	
Calories:	151	Milk:	0.0
Fat (gm):	0.9	Veg.:	1.0
Cholesterol (mg):	19	Fruit:	0.0
Sodium (mg):	224	Bread:	1.0
Potassium (mg):	806	Meat:	1.0
Sat. fat (gm):	0.1	Fat:	0.0
% Calories from fat:	6		

MAINE CLAM CHOWDER

Clam chowder can be served as a main dish. The succulent bits of clams give taste and texture to the chowder. Maine chowder is usually prepared with bacon, giving it a slightly smoky taste. If you wish, you can sprinkle the soup with a few dashes of bacon bits before serving.

8 Servings

32 Littleneck clams, or other fresh small clams, washed

Canola oil, or non-stick cooking spray

1 cup onions, chopped

½ cup celery, sliced

1 carrot, sliced thin

4 boiling potatoes, about 2 lbs., scrubbed, peeled, cubed

2 cups skim milk

½ cup clam juice

¼ cup all-purpose flour

¼ teaspoon white pepper

Wash clams and discard any that are open. Put closed clams in large saucepan; add 6 cups hot water. Cover and cook over medium heat 5 to 10 minutes or until clams open. Discard any clams that do not open. Remove clams from shell. Discard shells. Chop clams; reserve. Strain liquid through double layer of cheesecloth; set liquid aside.

Spray bottom of large pan or soup pot or coat lightly with oil. Saute onions, celery, carrot, and potatoes, covered, 5 minutes over medium heat. Stir occasionally. Add skim milk, reserved clam liquid, and clam juice. Cover and simmer 25 to 30 minutes or until all vegetables are tender.

Remove ½ cup of soup to small bowl. Whisk in flour and pepper. Stir flour mixture into chowder. Add chopped clams. Continue cooking until chowder thickens slightly.

Ladle chowder into bowls. Serve with chowder crackers if desired.

Nutritional Data

PER SERVING		EXCHANGES	
Calories:	163	Milk:	0.5
Fat (gm):	0.8	Veg.:	0.5
Cholesterol (mg):	20	Fruit:	0.0
Sodium (mg):	96	Bread:	1.5
Potassium (mg):	671	Meat:	0.0
Sat. fat (gm):	0.2	Fat:	0.0
% Calories from fat:	5		

Potato Fish Chowder

The fish called for in this chowder can be exchanged for fish of your choice or fish that is readily available. When I was vacationing in Maine, we always had a pot of fish chowder simmering on a back burner, adding more fish and milk as guests arrived. To make sure there aren't any bones, run you hand lightly over the fish; remove bones with a tweezers reserved for kitchen use.

8 Servings

- 1 teaspoon non-cholesterol margarine
- 1 cup onions, sliced
- ½ cup celery, sliced
- 3 boiling potatoes, about 1½ lbs., skin on, scrubbed, cubed
- 4 cups skim milk
- ⅛ teaspoon saffron
- ¼ teaspoon white pepper
- ½ lb. haddock or cod filets
- ¼ cup salad shrimp, washed

Melt margarine in large non-stick saucepan or stock pot. Saute onions, celery, and potatoes, covered, over medium heat, stirring occasionally, about 4 minutes. Mix in milk. Stir saffron with 1 tablespoon hot water for 5 minutes; drain and add saffron liquid to soup, discarding saffron threads. Mix in pepper.

Bring soup to boil. Reduce heat and simmer 30 minutes or until vegetables are tender. Add fish and shrimp. Continue cooking 5 minutes or until fish flakes easily when prodded with fork.

Stir soup occasionally. Taste to adjust seasonings. For a richer soup, add ½ cup clam juice.

Nutritional Data

PER SERVING		EXCHANGES	
Calories:	147	Milk:	0.5
Fat (gm):	0.9	Veg.:	0.0
Cholesterol (mg):	37	Fruit:	0.0
Sodium (mg):	119	Bread:	1.0
Potassium (mg):	611	Meat:	1.0
Sat. fat (gm):	0.3	Fat:	0.0
% Calories from fat:	6		

POTATO CURRY SOUP

Spice is the key to flavorful "skinny" cooking. In this recipe we use curry and cumin. They help accent the fresh flavor of the soup.

8 Servings

3 large boiling potatoes, about 1½ lbs.,
  scrubbed, peeled, sliced thin
  Olive oil, or non-stick cooking spray
1 cup green onions, chopped
3 cloves garlic
4 cups Chicken Stock (see Index)
1 can, 12 ozs., light skim milk
1 cup skim milk
¾ teaspoon curry powder
½ teaspoon ground cumin
¼ teaspoon pepper

over potatoes with water and bring to boil. Reduce heat to simmer and continue cooking until potatoes are fork tender. Drain.

Spray soup pot or other large pan or coat lightly with oil. Saute green onions and garlic, partially covered, over medium-low heat 4 minutes. Stir occasionally.

Add potatoes, chicken stock, skim milk, and spices. Simmer 20 minutes, stirring occasionally.

Ladle soup into individual bowls and serve hot.

Nutritional Data

PER SERVING		EXCHANGES	
Calories:	96	Milk:	0.5
Fat (gm):	0.2	Veg.:	1.0
Cholesterol (mg):	2	Fruit:	0.0
Sodium (mg):	69	Bread:	0.5
Potassium (mg):	427	Meat:	0.0
Sat. fat (gm):	0.1	Fat:	0.0
% Calories from fat:	2		

SUMMER POTATO BUTTERMILK SOUP

For best flavor use fresh dill. It is easy to grow your own herbs. Try growing them in pots in the kitchen or in a window box. They provide garden fresh flavors for summer soups.

8 Servings

- 3 boiling potatoes, about 1½ lbs., skin on, scrubbed
- 2 cups cucumber, peeled, seeded, chopped
- ¼ cup fresh dill, chopped
- 1 teaspoon dry mustard
- ½ teaspoon each ingredient: sugar, ground cumin
- 1 qt. buttermilk

lace potatoes in saucepan. Cover potatoes with water and bring to boil. Reduce heat to simmer and continue cooking until fork tender. Drain. Cool potatoes to room temperature and cube.

Using a large bowl, toss potatoes, cucumber, and dill. Mix in remaining ingredients. Taste to adjust seasonings.

Cover bowl lightly; chill before serving. Stir and serve soup cold. You may want to add a sprig of dill on top of each bowl of soup for garnish.

Nutritional Data

PER SERVING		EXCHANGES	
Calories:	105	Milk:	0.5
Fat (gm):	1.2	Veg.:	0.0
Cholesterol (mg):	18	Fruit:	0.0
Sodium (mg):	147	Bread:	1.0
Potassium (mg):	430	Meat:	0.0
Sat. fat (gm):	0.7	Fat:	0.0
% Calories from fat:	11		

BEET SOUP WITH POTATOES AND YOGURT

◆

This is one of our favorite family recipes, so how could I not include it. The concept of cold soup with hot potatoes is interesting and surprising; the flavors meld together unusually well.

◆

8 Servings

- 1½ lbs. beets, trimmed
- 2 teaspoons sugar
- 1 tablespoon red wine vinegar
- ¼ teaspoon pepper
- 4 baking potatoes, about 2 lbs., skin on, scrubbed
- 2 cups plain non-fat yogurt

ut beets in large saucepan and cover with water. Bring to boil, cover, and continue cooking about 35 minutes or until beets are done.

Drain and cool beets. When cool enough to handle, skin and slice beets. Puree in food processor fitted with steel blade.

Spoon beets into saucepan. Mix in 1 quart water, sugar, vinegar, and pepper. Bring mixture to boil; reduce heat to simmer. Continue cooking 30 minutes, stirring occasionally. Cool, pour soup into covered container, and chill several hours before serving.

Scrub potatoes and prick several times with sharp point of knife. Place potatoes on baking sheet and bake at 425°F. for 1 hour or until potato is fork tender. When potatoes are cool enough to handle, cut each in half horizontally and scoop out meat using a spoon. Mash hot potato pulp in bowl and bring to table hot.

Ladle soup into bowls. Serve with plain hot mashed potatoes and yogurt on the side. Instruct guests to put hot potatoes and yogurt into soup bowls. Good summer or winter.

◆

Nutritional Data

PER SERVING		EXCHANGES	
Calories:	127	Milk:	0.5
Fat (gm):	0.2	Veg.:	0.0
Cholesterol (mg):	1	Fruit:	0.0
Sodium (mg):	143	Bread:	1.5
Potassium (mg):	636	Meat:	0.0
Sat. fat (gm):	0.1	Fat:	0.0
% Calories from fat:	1		

◆

POTATO PISTOU

◆

The basil, garlic, and freshly grated Parmesan cheese is ground together to form a paste, then stirred into the soup before serving time. This makes a rich and flavorful soup.

◆

6 Servings

- 2 cups onions, chopped
- 4 boiling potatoes, peeled, diced
- 4 tomatoes, peeled, seeded, chopped
- ¾ cup green beans, trimmed, cut into 1½-inch pieces
- 2 medium zucchini, sliced
- 1 cup tomatoes, crushed
- ¼ teaspoon each ingredient: pepper, marjoram, saffron threads
- 1½ cups, firmly packed, basil leaves
- 5 cloves garlic
- ¼ cup Parmesan cheese, fresh-grated

 Pour 2 quarts water into soup pot; simmer onions and potatoes 35 minutes. Add tomatoes, green beans, zucchini, crushed tomatoes, pepper, and marjoram. Soak saffron in 1 tablespoon hot water for 5 minutes; drain and spoon flavored liquid into soup. Simmer 20 minutes.

Puree vegetables, then return them to clean pot. Bring soup to boil; reduce heat to simmer.

While soup is simmering, puree basil, garlic, and cheese in food processor fitted with steel blade. Blend the paste into soup. Ladle soup into individual bowls and serve hot.

◆

Nutritional Data

PER SERVING		EXCHANGES	
Calories:	163	Milk:	0.0
Fat (gm):	2	Veg.:	3.0
Cholesterol (mg):	3	Fruit:	0.0
Sodium (mg):	166	Bread:	1.0
Potassium (mg):	924	Meat:	0.0
Sat. fat (gm):	0.9	Fat:	0.5
% Calories from fat:	10		

GOULASH SOUP

This is our delicious variation of goulash. The beef has been eliminated, making it a vegetarian dish. But it is still a very flavorful soup.

8 Servings

Canola oil, or non-stick cooking spray
1 tablespoon non-cholesterol margarine
1½ cups onions, chopped
2 green bell peppers, seeded, sliced thin
3 carrots, sliced thin
1 large parsnip, sliced
1 cup celery, chopped
1 can tomato juice, 16 ozs.
2 large boiling potatoes, about 1 lb., scrubbed, peeled, chopped
¼ teaspoon paprika
1 teaspoon caraway seeds, or to taste
¼ teaspoon pepper

pray soup pot or other large pot or lightly coat with oil. Melt margarine. Saute onions, peppers, carrots, parsnip, celery, tomato juice, and potatoes, sprinkled with paprika, covered, about 5 minutes, stirring occasionally.

Add 1½ quarts water and remaining ingredients. Simmer 45 minutes to 1 hour or until all vegetables are tender. Serve soup hot. You might want to add a dollop of plain non-fat yogurt to top the soup before serving.

Nutritional Data

PER SERVING		EXCHANGES	
Calories:	102	Milk:	0.0
Fat (gm):	1	Veg.:	1.0
Cholesterol (mg):	0	Fruit:	0.0
Sodium (mg):	45	Bread:	1.0
Potassium (mg):	470	Meat:	0.0
Sat. fat (gm):	0.2	Fat:	0.0
% Calories from fat:	8		

Potato Barley Soup

Experiment with vegetables that are readily available or are your favorites. Most soups can be stored in refrigerator up to four days. As a matter of fact, many soups taste better after aging one day in the refrigerator.

8 Servings

Olive oil, or non-stick cooking spray
1 cup onions, chopped
3 cloves garlic, minced
3 cups boiling potatoes, peeled, diced
2 large carrots, sliced
3 ribs celery, sliced
1 parsnip, sliced
2 bay leaves
1 cup tomato juice
¾ cup barley
4 cups low-salt Vegetable Stock (see Index)
½ teaspoon each ingredient: salt, pepper, thyme, marjoram

 pray soup pot or coat lightly with oil. Saute onions, garlic, and potatoes 5 minutes, covered, stirring occasionally, over medium heat. Add remaining ingredients. Simmer, partially covered, 25 minutes or until vegetables and barley are tender, stirring occasionally. Discard bay leaves; taste to adjust seasonings. For a smoother taste, you can puree soup, reheat, and serve.

Nutritional Data

PER SERVING		EXCHANGES	
Calories:	149	Milk:	0.0
Fat (gm):	0.6	Veg.:	2.0
Cholesterol (mg):	0	Fruit:	0.0
Sodium (mg):	274	Bread:	1.5
Potassium (mg):	475	Meat:	0.0
Sat. fat (gm):	0.1	Fat:	0.0
% Calories from fat:	4		

4.
STIR-FRY POTATOES

Potatoes with Couscous

Sweet Potatoes, Beef, and Water Chestnuts

Potatoes and Asian Vegetables

Potatoes with Two Mushrooms

Potatoes and Spiced Bean Curd

Potato-Vegetable with Mustard Vinaigrette

Potatoes with Chicken and Peanuts

Potatoes with Chicken, Pea Pods, and Tomatoes

Potatoes with Salmon, Capers, and Dill

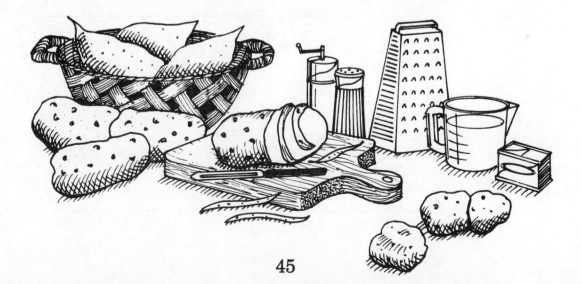

POTATO STIR-FRY WITH COUSCOUS

This is a slimmed down version of a usually rich dish. But it still captures the flavor without the caloric ingredients.

8 Servings

    4 boiling potatoes, 5–6 ozs. each, peeled, cut
       into ½-in. cubes
       Canola oil, or non-stick cooking spray
    1 tablespoon non-cholesterol margarine
    4 cloves garlic, minced
 1¼ cups red onions, thinly sliced
    3 cups button mushrooms, sliced
   ½ cup low-salt Chicken Stock (see Index)
   ½ cup cooked couscous
   ½ teaspoon cumin seeds
   ¼ teaspoon each ingredient: ground cumin,
       ground cinnamon, fresh-ground black pepper

lace cubed potatoes in saucepan; cover with water. Bring to boil over medium-high heat. Reduce heat to medium and continue cooking about 8 minutes or until potatoes are just fork tender. Drain.

Spray a non-stick wok, regular wok, or frying pan; or lightly coat with oil. Melt margarine. Stir-fry garlic, onions, mushrooms, potatoes, and stock, covered, until vegetables are just cooked. Stir occasionally.

Mix in couscous, cumin seeds, and seasonings. Serve hot.

Nutritional Data

PER SERVING		EXCHANGES	
Calories:	98	Milk:	0.0
Fat (gm):	1.1	Veg.:	1.0
Cholesterol (mg):	0	Fruit:	0.0
Sodium (mg):	26	Bread:	1.0
Potassium (mg):	375	Meat:	0.0
Sat. fat (gm):	0.2	Fat:	0.0
% Calories from fat:	10		

STIR-FRY SWEET POTATOES, BEEF, AND WATER CHESTNUTS

Sweet potatoes add a richness and unique flavor to this oriental-style dish. White potatoes can be substituted. To grate ginger, cut off the dry end and peel back the skin with a small, sharp knife. Grate the ginger, using the fine side of a hand grater, a food processor fitted with steel blade, or a small oriental hand grater, which is available at most oriental grocery stores.

8 Servings

- 4 sweet potatoes, 5–6 ozs. each, peeled, cut into ½-in. cubes
  Canola oil, or non-stick cooking spray
- 1 tablespoon non-cholesterol margarine
- 4 cloves garlic, minced
- ½ teaspoon ginger, fresh-grated
- 8 green onions, trimmed, cut in half lengthwise, sliced into 1½-in. pieces
- ½ cup low-salt Vegetable Stock (see Index)
- 5-6 ozs. flank steak, chilled to slice easily, across the grain, into ⅛-in. strips
- 1 can, 8 ozs., sliced water chestnuts, drained
- 2 cups broccoli, cut up
- 2 teaspoons cornstarch, mixed with 2 tablespoons water
- 2 tablespoon oyster sauce
- ¼ teaspoon black pepper fresh-ground

 lace cubed potatoes in saucepan; cover with water. (If potatoes are to stand for any length of time, place them in a glass bowl and cover with cold water. Drain well and pat dry with paper towels before using.) Bring potatoes to boil over medium-high heat. Reduce heat to medium and cook about 8 minutes or until potatoes are just fork tender. Drain.

Spray a non-stick wok, regular wok, or frying pan; or lightly coat with oil. Melt margarine. Stir-fry garlic, ginger, onions, and potatoes over medium heat, stirring occasionally. Add stock as you cook, stirring occasionally. It might be necessary to add more liquid, stock or water, by the tablespoon to prevent potatoes from sticking to bottom of pan.

Add steak, water chestnuts, and broccoli. Stir-fry over high heat until beef loses its color. Add cornstarch mixture, oyster sauce, and pepper. Stir to combine.

Spoon mixture into bowls and serve hot.

Nutritional Data

PER SERVING		EXCHANGES	
Calories:	135	Milk:	0.0
Fat (gm):	2.7	Veg.:	1.0
Cholesterol (mg):	10	Fruit:	0.0
Sodium (mg):	80	Bread:	1.0
Potassium (mg):	367	Meat:	0.5
Sat. fat (gm):	0.9	Fat:	0.0
% Calories from fat:	18		

STIR-FRY POTATOES AND ASIAN VEGETABLES

◆

The Asian vegetables that we use in this recipe are bok choy, bamboo shoots, bean sprouts, and reconstituted shiitaki mushrooms. As we say in so many of the recipes, feel free to exchange the vegetables for ones that are on hand or that you prefer.

◆

8 Servings

4 boiling potatoes, 5–6 ozs. each, peeled, cut into ½-in. cubes
   Canola oil, or non-stick cooking spray
4 cloves garlic, minced
½ teaspoon ginger root, grated
1 cup green onions, chopped
1 tablespoon cornstarch, mixed with 2 tablespoons water
½ cup low-salt Chicken Stock (see Index)
3 cups bok choy, sliced
8 shiitaki mushrooms, reconstituted in hot water for 20 minutes, drained, sliced
2 cups bean sprouts, rinsed under hot running water
2 tablespoons light soy sauce
½ teaspoon curry powder
½ teaspoon black pepper, fresh-ground.

Cube potatoes. If not using potatoes immediately, set them in bowl of cold water. When ready to use, place in saucepan and cover with water. Bring to boil over medium-high heat. Reduce heat to medium and continue cooking about 8 minutes or until potatoes are just fork tender. Drain.

Spray a non-stick wok, regular wok or frying pan; or lightly coat with oil. Stir-fry garlic, ginger, and green onions, covered, about 3 minutes or until vegetables are tender. Stir occasionally.

Add potatoes and stir-fry, covered, over high heat until just cooked and beginning to brown. Add cornstarch mixture and stock. Stir occasionally to prevent potatoes from sticking to bottom of pan.

Stir in remaining vegetables, one at a time. Sprinkle with soy sauce, curry powder, and pepper. Stir-fry until vegetables are hot and only just cooked. Do not overcook vegetables; they should be crunchy.

Spoon stir-fry into serving bowl, and bring to table hot. Good as a side dish or main dish.

Nutritional Data

PER SERVING		EXCHANGES	
Calories:	95	Milk:	0.0
Fat (gm):	0.2	Veg.:	1.0
Cholesterol (mg):	0	Fruit:	0.0
Sodium (mg):	152	Bread:	1.0
Potassium (mg):	411	Meat:	0.0
Sat. fat (gm):	0	Fat:	0.0
% Calories from fat:	2		

POTATOES STIR-FRY WITH TWO MUSHROOMS

Potatoes and mushrooms make a perfect marriage of flavors and textures for this stir-fry.

8 Servings

4 boiling potatoes, 5–6 ozs. each, skin on, cut into ½-in. cubes
  Olive oil, on non-stick cooking spray
1 tablespoon non-cholesterol margarine
2 cups leeks, sliced, white part only, washed well
2 cups button mushrooms, sliced
1½ cups brown mushrooms, sliced, or other mushrooms of choice
½ cup low-salt Chicken Stock (see Index), or water
1½ tablespoons cornstarch, mixed with 2 tablespoons water
½ teaspoon tarragon
¼ teaspoon black pepper, fresh-ground

 Place cubed potatoes in saucepan, cover with water, and bring to boil over medium-high heat. Reduce heat to medium and continue cooking about 8 minutes or until potatoes are just fork tender. Drain.

Spray a non-stick wok, regular wok or frying pan; or lightly coat with oil. Melt margarine. Stir-fry leeks, mushrooms, and potatoes about 6 minutes or until they are tender. Stir occasionally.

Add stock to prevent potatoes from sticking to pan. Stir in cornstarch mixture. Sprinkle with tarragon and pepper. Continue cooking until vegetables are just cooked and hot.

Spoon stir-fry into deep serving bowl; serve hot.

Nutritional Data

PER SERVING		EXCHANGES	
Calories:	120	Milk:	0.0
Fat (gm):	1	Veg.:	2.0
Cholesterol (mg):	0	Fruit:	0.0
Sodium (mg):	31	Bread:	1.0
Potassium (mg):	504	Meat:	0.0
Sat. fat (gm):	0.2	Fat:	0.0
% Calories from fat:	8		

STIR-FRY POTATOES AND SPICED BEAN CURD

Spicy food lovers will enjoy this new twist to a tofu-potato stir-fry. One of the advantages of cooking with potatoes in the stir-fry is that it makes a complete meal in a very short time. The dishes never have to be the same twice. Just use your imagination and leftovers that go together and you enjoy.

8 Servings

4 boiling potatoes, 5–6 ozs. each, skin on, scrubbed, cut into ½-in. cubes
  Canola oil, or non-stick cooking spray
1 tablespoon non-cholesterol margarine
2 cloves garlic, minced
½ teaspoon ginger root, grated
6 green onions, trimmed, cut lengthwise, and then into 1½-in pieces
8 ozs. firm bean curd, drained, cut into ¾-in. pieces
½ cup crushed tomatoes, include juice
1 tablespoon dry white wine
2 tablespoons light soy sauce
½ teaspoon red pepper flakes, or 1 teaspoon Szechwan chili bean sauce, available at oriental grocery stores
¼ teaspoon cayenne pepper
⅓ cup low-salt Chicken Stock (see Index)
1 tablespoon cornstarch, mixed with 2 tablespoons water

lace cubed potatoes in saucepan; cover with water. (If potatoes are to stand for any length of time, place them in a glass bowl and cover with cold water. Drain well and pat dry with paper towels before using.) Bring potatoes to boil over medium-high heat. Reduce heat to medium and cook about 8 minutes or until potatoes are just fork tender. Drain.

Spray a non-stick wok, regular wok or frying pan; or lightly coat with oil. Melt margarine. Stir-fry potatoes, garlic, ginger, and green onions over medium-high heat, partially covered, 2 minutes, stirring occasionally.

Gently stir in bean curd, crushed tomatoes, wine, soy sauce, red pepper flakes, and cayenne pepper. Mix in stock and cornstarch mixture. Continue cooking only until stock thickens slightly.

Spoon stir-fry into serving bowl, and bring to table hot.

Nutritional Data

PER SERVING		EXCHANGES	
Calories:	132	Milk:	0.0
Fat (gm):	3.3	Veg.:	1.0
Cholesterol (mg):	0	Fruit:	0.0
Sodium (mg):	199	Bread:	1.0
Potassium (mg):	429	Meat:	0.5
Sat. fat (gm):	0.5	Fat:	0.0
% Calories from fat:	21		

POTATO-VEGETABLE STIR-FRY WITH MUSTARD VINAIGRETTE

For your personal convenience, use vegetables that are in season. This recipe is a perfect fall root vegetable stir-fry.

8 Servings

4 boiling potatoes, 5–6 ozs. each, peeled, cut into ½-in. cubes
  Olive oil, or non-stick cooking spray
1 tablespoon non-cholesterol margarine
4 large shallots, sliced thin
2 large leeks, washed well, use white part only, sliced thin
¾ cup turnip, thinly sliced, blanched
2 large carrots, sliced thin
½ cup low-salt Chicken Stock (see Index)

Mustard Vinaigrette
1½ tablespoons stone-ground mustard
¾ cup plain non-fat yogurt
3 tablespoons red wine vinegar
1 teaspoon basil
12 teaspoons garlic powder
¼ teaspoon each ingredient: salt, fresh-ground black pepper

C ube potatoes, place in saucepan, cover with water, and bring to boil. Reduce heat to medium and continue cooking about 8 minutes or until potatoes are just fork tender. Drain.

Spray a non-stick wok, regular wok, or frying pan; or lightly coat with oil. Melt margarine. Stir-fry shallots, leeks, and turnips, covered, 3 minutes, stirring occasionally. Add well-drained potatoes, carrots, and stock. Cover and continue cooking, stirring occasionally, about 2 to 4 minutes or until vegetables are tender. Add extra stock or water by the tablespoon if needed to prevent vegetables from sticking to bottom of pan.

While vegetables are cooking, prepare vinaigrette by mixing all ingredients together in small bowl.

Spoon vegetables into large serving bowl. Toss vegetables with dressing. Taste to adjust seasonings. Serve hot as a main dish.

Nutritional Data

PER SERVING		EXCHANGES	
Calories:	121	Milk:	0.0
Fat (gm):	1	Veg.:	2.0
Cholesterol (mg):	0	Fruit:	0.0
Sodium (mg):	123	Bread:	1.0
Potassium (mg):	502	Meat:	0.0
Sat. fat (gm):	0.2	Fat:	0.0
% Calories from fat:	7		

POTATO STIR-FRY WITH CHICKEN AND PEANUTS

This is a good recipe for a fast, hearty winter dinner or lunch. Remember that the amount of red pepper flakes is to taste. For those who prefer a more intense dish, simply increase the red pepper flakes.

8 Servings

4 boiling potatoes, 5–6 ozs. each, skin on, cut into ½-in. cubes

Canola oil, or non-stick cooking spray

1 tablespoon non-cholesterol margarine

4 cloves garlic, minced

½ teaspoon powdered ginger

¾ cup green onions, cut into 1½-in. slices

¼ teaspoon red pepper flakes, or to taste

1 large green or red bell pepper, cut into 1-in. slices

1 small chicken breast, about 4 ozs., boned, skinned, cubed

2 egg whites, slightly beaten

½ cup low-salt Chicken Stock (see Index), or water

1 can, 8 ozs., sliced bamboo shoots, drained

1 tablespoon cornstarch, mixed with 2 tablespoons water

3 tablespoons catsup

1 tablespoon light soy sauce

¼ teaspoon pepper

Place cubed potatoes in saucepan, cover with water, and bring to boil over medium-high heat. Reduce heat to medium and continue cooking about 8 minutes or until potatoes are just fork tender. Drain.

Spray a non-stick wok, regular wok, or frying pan; or lightly coat with oil. Melt margarine. Stir-fry garlic, ginger, onions, pepper flakes, and bell pepper slices, covered, 3 to 4 minutes or until vegetables are just tender. Stir occasionally.

Toss chicken with slightly beaten egg whites; add chicken and potatoes to vegetables. Stir-fry about 3 minutes. Stir in stock and stir-fry, covered about 3 minutes or until potatoes are beginning to brown and chicken is cooked. Mix in bamboo shoots and remaining ingredients. Taste to adjust flavor.

Spoon stir-fry into deep serving bowl, and bring to table hot.

Nutritional Data

PER SERVING		EXCHANGES	
Calories:	123	Milk:	0.0
Fat (gm):	1.7	Veg.:	1.0
Cholesterol (mg):	6	Fruit:	0.0
Sodium (mg):	183	Bread:	1.0
Potassium (mg):	238	Meat:	0.5
Sat. fat (gm):	0.3	Fat:	0.0
% Calories from fat:	12		

POTATO STIR-FRY WITH CHICKEN, PEA PODS, AND TOMATOES

To stir-fry potatoes cook the cubed potatoes first, drain, and add them to the remaining ingredients according to the individual recipe.

8 Servings

- 4 boiling potatoes, 5–6 ozs. each, skin on, cut into ½-in. cubes
  Canola oil, or non-stick cooking spray
- 3 cloves garlic, minced
- 1 cup green onions, chopped
- ½ teaspoon powdered ginger
- ½ cup low-salt Vegetable Stock (see Index)
- 1 chicken breast, 5–6 ozs., skinned, boned, thinly sliced
- 2 cups pea pods, trimmed
- 1½ cups thin tomato wedges
- 1½ tablespoons light soy sauce
- 1 teaspoon sugar
- 2 tablespoons white wine

P lace cubed potatoes in saucepan, cover with water, and bring to boil over medium-high heat. Reduce to medium heat and continue cooking about 8 minutes or until potatoes are just fork tender. Drain.

Spray a non-stick wok, regular wok, or frying pan; or lightly coat with oil. Stir-fry garlic, onions, and ginger, covered, until vegetables are tender. Stir occasionally.

Add stock, chicken, and pea pods. Stir-fry until chicken is cooked. Add potatoes and remaining ingredients. Stir to combine and heat food. Spoon stir-fry into serving bowl and bring to table hot.

Nutritional Data

PER SERVING		EXCHANGES	
Calories:	114	Milk:	0.0
Fat (gm):	0.5	Veg.:	2.0
Cholesterol (mg):	7	Fruit:	0.0
Sodium (mg):	127	Bread:	1.0
Potassium (mg):	419	Meat:	0.0
Sat. fat (gm):	0.1	Fat:	0.0
% Calories from fat:	4		

STIR-FRY POTATOES WITH SALMON, CAPERS, AND DILL

8 Servings

 4 boiling potatoes, 5–6 ozs. each, skin on, cut
   into ½-in. cubes
   Olive oil, or non-stick cooking spray
 1 tablespoon non-cholesterol margarine
 1 cup red onions, chopped
 3 cloves garlic, minced
¼–⅓ cup low-salt Vegetable Stock (see Index)
 1 red or green bell pepper, seeded, sliced thin
 1 can salmon, 14¾ ozs., drained, flaked
 1 tablespoon capers, drained
 ¼ teaspoon black pepper, fresh-ground
 ½ cup fresh dill, chopped

 lace cubed potatoes in saucepan; cover with water. (If potatoes
are to stand for any length of time, place them in a glass bowl
and cover with cold water. Drain well and pat dry with paper towels
before using.) Bring potatoes to boil over medium-high heat. Reduce heat
to medium and cook about 8 minutes or until potatoes are just fork
tender. Drain.

Spray a non-stick wok, regular wok, or frying pan; or lightly coat
with oil. Melt margarine. Stir-fry garlic, onions, potatoes, and stock,
covered, stirring occasionally until vegetables are tender, over medium-
high heat. Cook 2 to 3 minutes.

Add extra vegetable stock as necessary to prevent potatoes from
sticking to pan. Add bell pepper and salmon. Stir-fry only until combined
and hot.

Spoon stir-fry into serving bowl, sprinkle with capers, fresh-ground
black pepper, and dill. Serve hot with crisp salad.

Nutritional Data

PER SERVING		EXCHANGES	
Calories:	156	Milk:	0.0
Fat (gm):	3.7	Veg.:	1.0
Cholesterol (mg):	25	Fruit:	0.0
Sodium (mg):	278	Bread:	1.0
Potassium (mg):	529	Meat:	1.0
Sat. fat (gm):	0.9	Fat:	0.0
% Calories from fat:	21		

5.
BAKED POTATOES
WITH TOPPINGS

Baked Potato Party

Shrimp and Asparagus

Tofu Veracruzana

Indian-Flavored Vegetables

Eggplant Parmesan

Thai Shrimp

Tomatoes and Melted Cheese

Mandarin Oranges and Cheese

Potato Ratatouille

Moroccan Chicken

Turkey Chili

Provençal Vegetables

Niçoise Salad

Vegetable Fajitas

Indian Chickpeas and Tomatoes

Cantonese Stir-Fry

Stir-Fried Hoisin Vegetables

Spanakopita Baked Potatoes

Mushrooms and Cheese

Curry Jacket Potatoes

Vegetable Chili

Chicken with Mustard

Chicken Fajitas

Sauteed Asparagus and Mushrooms

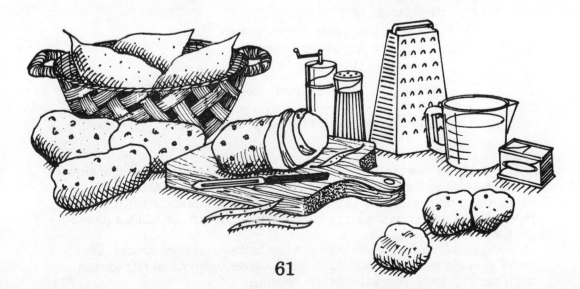

61

BAKED POTATO PARTY

What fun to have a baked potato party after a football game or a get together. The baked potatoes, cooked to perfection, are served hot with sauces and toppings. Let your guests help themselves. This recipe can easily be doubled to accommodate more guests.

8 Servings

4 baking potatoes, 5–6 ozs. each, skin on, scrubbed

Pineapple Salsa (makes about 2¼ cups)

1 bunch green onions, chopped

3 jalapeño chilies, seeded, minced (wear rubber gloves when preparing hot peppers)

1 large red bell pepper, seeded, chopped

½ cup unsweetened, crushed pineapple, drained

½ cup cilantro, chopped

2 red tomatoes, chopped

2 cloves garlic, minced

½ teaspoon ground cumin

Caponata (makes about 2 cups)

1 eggplant, ¾–1 lb., pricked with fork or knife

¾ cup red onion, chopped

⅓ cup parsley, minced

2 cloves garlic, minced

1½ tablespoons capers, drained

¾ teaspoon basil

½ teaspoon oregano

3 tablespoons green olives, minced

1 tablespoon fresh lemon juice

1 teaspoon olive oil

1 cup plain non-fat yogurt, spooned into serving bowl

Shakers of garlic powder, ground nutmeg, basil, oregano

P reheat oven to 425°F. Scrub potatoes and stick with tip of sharp knife or fork several times. Set potatoes on non-stick cookie sheet. Bake on center rack of oven 45 minutes to 1 hour or until cooked. Potatoes are done when a knife inserted will test soft, or when squeezed gently will "give" slightly.

Pineapple Salsa: While potatoes are baking, prepare sauces. To make salsa, mix all ingredients in bowl. Cover lightly and refrigerate until serving time. Stir salsa before serving.

Caponata: Bake eggplant at 375°F. until soft, or microwave eggplant on double thickness of paper towels, uncovered, on High 10 to 12 minutes or until eggplant is soft. Cool. When eggplant is cool enough to handle, cut in half, and use spoon to scoop out meat. Puree eggplant. In deep bowl, mix eggplant with remaining ingredients. Cover lightly and refrigerate until serving time. Stir before serving.

Cut hot baked potatoes in half horizontally and gently squeeze open. Place potatoes on serving dish or on tray and serve. Put Salsa and Caponata on table along with yogurt and shakers of seasonings. Enjoy!

Nutritional Data with Pineapple Salsa

PER SERVING		EXCHANGES	
Calories:	94	Milk:	0.0
Fat (gm):	0.3	Veg.:	1.0
Cholesterol (mg):	0	Fruit:	0.0
Sodium (mg):	56	Bread:	1.0
Potassium (mg):	456	Meat:	0.0
Sat. fat (gm):	0	Fat:	0.0
% Calories from fat:	3		

Nutritional Data with Caponata

PER SERVING		EXCHANGES	
Calories:	97	Milk:	0.0
Fat (gm):	1	Veg.:	1.0
Cholesterol (mg):	0	Fruit:	0.0
Sodium (mg):	14	Bread:	1.0
Potassium (mg):	434	Meat:	0.0
Sat. fat (gm):	0.1	Fat:	0.0
% Calories from fat:	9		

SHRIMP AND ASPARAGUS OVER BAKED POTATOES

To reconstitute oriental or other dried mushrooms, cover them with boiling water, let stand 30 minutes, and drain. Squeeze out excess water.

8 Servings

4 baking potatoes, 5–6 ozs. each, skin on, scrubbed
  Canola oil, or non-stick cooking spray
½ teaspoon ginger root, grated
3 cups thin asparagus, cut into 2-in. pieces, blanched
2 cups bok choy, sliced thin
½ cup dried oriental shiitaki mushrooms, reconstituted, drained
1 cup low-salt Chicken Stock (see Index)
1 tablespoon cornstarch
½ teaspoon sugar
1 tablespoon dry white wine
¼ cup shrimp, peeled, chopped

P reheat oven to 425°F. Scrub potatoes and stick with tip of sharp knife or fork several times. Set potatoes on non-stick cookie sheet. Bake on center rack of oven 45 minutes to 1 hour or until cooked. Potatoes are done when a knife inserted will test soft, or when squeezed gently will "give" slightly.

While potatoes are baking, prepare vegetables and sauce. Spray a non-stick wok, or frying pan; or lightly coat with oil. Cook ginger, asparagus, bok choy, and mushrooms over medium-high heat, covered. Stir often until vegetables are just heated, not soggy.

Whisk together chicken stock and cornstarch. Stir in stock mixture, sugar, wine, and shrimp. Reduce heat to simmer and continue cooking until hot, about 1 minute.

To serve, cut hot baked potatoes in half horizontally and gently squeeze open. Spoon vegetables over potatoes and serve hot.

Nutritional Data

PER SERVING		EXCHANGES	
Calories:	111	Milk:	0.0
Fat (gm):	0.4	Veg.:	1.0
Cholesterol (mg):	8	Fruit:	0.0
Sodium (mg):	21	Bread:	1.0
Potassium (mg):	514	Meat:	0.0
Sat. fat (gm):	0.1	Fat:	0.0
% Calories from fat:	3		

Tofu Veracruzana over Baked Potatoes

Both baking and roasting are dry-heat methods in which food is usually placed in a pan and cooked in the oven. There is no real difference between the two cooking methods; the word "baking" is used for vegetables while "roasting" is used for poultry, beef, or lamb. Veracruz-style dishes are classically served with sliced potatoes in the sauce. For this recipe, the potato is not in the sauce but rather the sauce is spooned over the potato.

8 Servings

- 4 baking potatoes, 5–6 ozs. each, skin on, scrubbed
  Olive oil, or non-stick cooking spray
- 2 cloves garlic, minced
- 1 cup onions, thinly sliced
- 1 green bell pepper, sliced
- 4 tomatoes, peeled, seeded, coarsely chopped
- 2 cups firm bean curd, cut into ½-in. pieces
- 1 bay leaf
- 1 tablespoon capers, drained
- 1 tablespoon black olives, chopped
- ½ teaspoon oregano
- ¼ teaspoon pepper

reheat oven to 425°F. Scrub potatoes and stick several times with tip of sharp knife or fork. Set potatoes on non-stick cookie sheet. Bake on center rack of oven 45 minutes to 1 hour or until cooked. Potatoes are done when a knife inserted will test soft, or when squeezed gently will "give" slightly.

While potatoes are baking prepare Veracruz sauce. Spray a non-stick saucepan, or lightly coat with oil. Saute garlic and onions, covered, over medium heat until onions are soft. Stir onions occasionally so they do not stick to bottom of pan. Add remaining ingredients and simmer, uncovered, 8 to 10 minutes.

Cut hot baked potatoes in half horizontally and gently squeeze open. Place potato halves on plates. Spoon Tofu Veracruz over potatoes and serve hot.

Nutritional Data

PER SERVING		EXCHANGES	
Calories:	189	Milk:	0.0
Fat (gm):	6	Veg.:	1.0
Cholesterol (mg):	0	Fruit:	0.0
Sodium (mg):	24	Bread:	1.0
Potassium (mg):	642	Meat:	1.0
Sat. fat (gm):	0.9	Fat:	0.0
% Calories from fat:	27		

Indian-Flavored Vegetables over Baked Potatoes

It is the marriage of Indian spices that gives this sauce its unique flavor. It is easy to prepare toppings to serve over perfectly baked potatoes. The children will love the change.

8 Servings

- 4 baking potatoes, 5–6 ozs. each, skin on, scrubbed
- Olive oil, or non-stick cooking spray
- 1 tablespoon margarine
- ½ teaspoon garlic powder
- ½ cup green onions, chopped
- 1 eggplant, about 1 lb., peeled, cubed
- 2 cups cauliflower, chopped, partially cooked
- 1¼ cups low-salt Chicken Stock (see Index)
- ½ teaspoon each ingredient: powdered ginger, dry mustard, tumeric
- ¼ teaspoon red pepper flakes
- 1 cup green peas, fresh or defrosted

P reheat oven to 425°F. Scrub potatoes and stick several times with tip of sharp knife or fork. Set potatoes on non-stick cookie sheet. Bake on center rack of oven 45 minutes to 1 hour or until cooked. Potatoes are done when a knife inserted will test soft, or when squeezed gently will "give" slightly.

While potatoes are baking prepare vegetables. Spray a non-stick frying pan; or lightly coat with oil. Melt margarine and add garlic, green onions, eggplant, cauliflower, and chicken stock. Cover and cook over medium heat until vegetables are fork tender, stirring occasionally. Remove cover and add remaining ingredients. Stir to combine vegetables; continue cooking only until hot.

Cut hot baked potatoes in half horizontally and gently squeeze open. Spoon vegetables over potatoes and serve hot.

Nutritional Data

PER SERVING		EXCHANGES	
Calories:	115	Milk:	0.0
Fat (gm):	1	Veg.:	0.5
Cholesterol (mg):	0	Fruit:	0.0
Sodium (mg):	43	Bread:	1.5
Potassium (mg):	558	Meat:	0.0
Sat. fat (gm):	0.2	Fat:	0.0
% Calories from fat:	8		

EGGPLANT PARMESAN OVER BAKED POTATOES

◆

There are low-cholesterol and low-sodium Parmesan cheeses on the market that will even melt slightly. Some cheeses taste better and melt better than others. Try them until you find one that you like. It is worth the effort.

◆

8 Servings

4 baking potatoes, 5–6 ozs. each, skin on, scrubbed
1 eggplant, about 1 lb., unpeeled, sliced thin
  Olive oil, or non-stick cooking spray
1 can, 16 ozs., crushed tomatoes, include juice
1 tablespoon balsamic vinegar
1 cup onions, chopped
1 teaspoon each ingredient: basil, oregano
¼ teaspoon pepper
¼ cup low-cholesterol Parmesan cheese, grated

Preheat oven to 425°F. Scrub potatoes and stick several times with tip of sharp knife or fork. Set potatoes on non-stick cookie sheet. Bake on center rack of oven 45 minutes to 1 hour or until cooked. Potatoes are done when a knife inserted will test soft, or when squeezed gently will "give" slightly.

To prepare eggplant, sprinkle with salt and let stand 30 minutes over double layer of paper towels; rinse under cold running water to remove salt; pat dry.

Spray a large non-stick frying pan; or lightly coat with oil. Saute eggplant over medium heat until cooked. Eggplant is cooked when fork tender and golden brown on both sides. Turn eggplant once or twice.

Transfer eggplant to non-stick casserole that has been sprayed. Set aside.

Using a medium-heavy saucepan, combine tomatoes, onions, vinegar, basil, oregano, and pepper. Bring sauce to boil, reduce heat to simmer, and continue cooking 5–10 minutes, stirring occasionally.

Spoon sauce over eggplant. Bake casserole 5 to 6 minutes in preheated 375°F. oven.

Cut hot baked potatoes in half horizontally and gently squeeze open. Place potato halves on non-stick cookie sheet. With a spatula, place a slice of eggplant, with sauce, over each potato half. Sprinkle with Parmesan cheese. Bake 5 minutes.

Remove potatoes to individual plates and serve hot. This is a good party dish.

Nutritional Data

PER SERVING		EXCHANGES	
Calories:	119	Milk:	0.0
Fat (gm):	0.9	Veg.:	2.0
Cholesterol (mg):	0	Fruit:	0.0
Sodium (mg):	168	Bread:	1.0
Potassium (mg):	610	Meat:	0.0
Sat. fat (gm):	0.3	Fat:	0.0
% Calories from fat:	6		

THAI SHRIMP OVER BAKED POTATOES

Thai restaurants have become popular due to their lovely tastes and flavors. Here we have a Thai-flavored sauce with baby shrimp to serve over hot baked potatoes. If you do not eat shrimp, substitute tofu or pea pods and tomato wedges.

8 Servings

4 baking potatoes, 5–6 ozs. each, skin on, scrubbed

Thai Sauce

1 tablespoon margarine
2 cloves garlic, minced
½ teaspoon ginger root, grated
½ cup tomato sauce
2 tablespoons light brown sugar
3 tablespoons pineapple juice
1 tablespoon red wine vinegar
⅛ teaspoon ground allspice
¾ lb. baby shrimp, washed, peeled, patted dry
1 cup lettuce or red cabbage, shredded
½ cup green onions, chopped

Preheat oven to 425°F. Scrub potatoes and stick several times with tip of sharp knife or fork. Set potatoes on non-stick cookie sheet. Bake on center rack of oven 45 minutes to 1 hour or until cooked. Potatoes are done when a knife inserted will test soft, or when squeezed gently will "give" slightly.

Thai Sauce: While potatoes are baking, prepare sauce and shrimp. Melt margarine in non-stick saucepan. Saute garlic and ginger about 30 seconds over medium heat. Add remaining ingredients except shrimp, lettuce and onions. Continue cooking over low heat about 2 minutes or until sauce is warm, stirring occasionally. Mix in shrimp and cook only until shrimp change from translucent to opaque. Do not overcook shrimp or they will become tough.

Cut hot baked potatoes in half horizontally and gently squeeze open. Place potato halves on plates, and spoon shrimp with sauce over them. Sprinkle with shredded lettuce and green onions. Serve hot.

Nutritional Data

PER SERVING		EXCHANGES	
Calories:	136	Milk:	0.0
Fat (gm):	1.2	Veg.:	0.5
Cholesterol (mg):	65	Fruit:	0.0
Sodium (mg):	190	Bread:	1.0
Potassium (mg):	469	Meat:	1.0
Sat. fat (gm):	0.3	Fat:	0.0
% Calories from fat:	8		

TOMATO AND MELTED CHEESE OVER BAKED POTATOES

"Baked" potatoes can be successfully cooked in the microwave. For a single potato, scrub well and prick several times with a knife; position it on a double thickness of paper towels, a paper plate, or a dish. Microwave the potato on High 7 to 10 minutes, depending on the size of the potato and the power of the individual microwave.

8 Servings

- 4 baking potatoes, 5–6 ozs. each, skin on, scrubbed
  Olive oil, or non-stick cooking spray
- 4 ozs. low-cholesterol cheese, such as Alpine lace, grated
- 1 can, 16 ozs., crushed tomatoes, reserve liquid
- ¾ cup red onions, chopped
- 1 green or red bell pepper, chopped
- ½ teaspoon chili powder
- ⅛ teaspoon cayenne pepper

Preheat oven to 425°F. Scrub potatoes and stick them several times with tip of sharp knife or fork. Set potatoes on non-stick cookie sheet. Bake them on center rack of oven 45 minutes to 1 hour or until cooked. Potatoes are cooked when a knife inserted will test soft, or when squeezed gently will "give" slightly.

While potatoes are baking, prepare cheese and tomato sauce. Spray a non-stick frying pan; or lightly coat with oil. Add cheese, tomatoes, onions, bell pepper, chili powder, and cayenne pepper to pan. Simmer, uncovered, 5 minutes or until cheese has melted and vegetables are hot.

Cut potatoes in half horizontally and gently squeeze open. Place potato halves on plates, and spoon cheese and tomato sauce over them. Serve hot.

Nutritional Data

PER SERVING		EXCHANGES	
Calories:	117	Milk:	0.0
Fat (gm):	1.3	Veg.:	1.0
Cholesterol (mg):	0	Fruit:	0.0
Sodium (mg):	237	Bread:	1.0
Potassium (mg):	540	Meat:	0.5
Sat. fat (gm):	0.5	Fat:	0.0
% Calories from fat:	9		

Baked Sweet Potatoes with Mandarin Oranges and Cheese Topping

Sweet potatoes contain vitamins A and C plus potassium and iron, yet they have only a trace of fat. In choosing sweet potatoes, look for those that are free from blemishes and heavy for their size.

To microwave a sweet potato, pierce it with a knife in several places. Position on a double layer of paper towels, and cook on High about 5 minutes, for a medium potato, or until the potato is cooked.

8 Servings

- 4 sweet potatoes, 5–6 ozs. each, skin on, scrubbed
- 2 cups non-fat ricotta cheese, or non-fat small-curd cottage cheese, well mixed
- 1 can, 8 ozs., mandarin oranges, reserve 2 tablespoons of liquid
- 1 cup banana, sliced
- 1 tablespoon lime juice, fresh-squeezed
- ½ teaspoon ground cinnamon
- ⅛ teaspoon ground allspice
- 2 tablespoons sugar

Preheat oven to 425°F. Scrub potatoes and stick them several times with tip of sharp knife or fork. Set potatoes on non-stick cookie sheet. Bake on center rack of oven 45 minutes to 1 hour or until potatoes are cooked. Potatoes are done when a knife inserted will test soft, or when squeezed gently will "give" slightly.

While potatoes are baking, prepare topping. In a mixing bowl, beat cheese until smooth. Mix in remaining ingredients. Refrigerate until serving time. Stir before serving; taste to adjust flavoring. If you want to increase sweetness, stir in reserved liquid from oranges.

When ready to serve, cut hot potatoes horizontally and gently squeeze open. Place potato halves on serving plate, and spoon cheese-fruit topping over them. Serve hot.

Nutritional Data

PER SERVING			EXCHANGES	
Calories:	178		Milk:	0.0
Fat (gm):	0.2		Veg.:	1.0
Cholesterol (mg):	6		Fruit:	0.0
Sodium (mg):	37		Bread:	1.0
Potassium (mg):	309		Meat:	1.0
Sat. fat (gm):	0.1		Fat:	0.0
% Calories from fat:	1			

POTATO RATATOUILLE

By combining classic ratatouille with thin-sliced potatoes, we have a recipe that is hardy enough for a complete meal. Potatoes add body to this already favorite mélange of vegetables.

8 Servings

3 cups boiling potatoes, peeled, partially cooked, drained, thinly sliced

1 large eggplant, ends cut off, skin on, cubed
Olive oil, or non-stick cooking spray

1 tablespoon non-cholesterol margarine

2 cloves garlic, minced

1 large red or white onion, thinly sliced

2 cups zucchini, thinly sliced

2 large red bell peppers, seeded, thinly sliced

1 can, 28 ozs. crushed tomatoes, include juice

¾ teaspoon basil

½ teaspoon oregano

¼ teaspoon each ingredient: salt, pepper

artially cook potatoes, covered in water, until just fork tender. Drain and cool 15 minutes. Sprinkle eggplant with 1 tablespoon salt; let stand 15 minutes, then wash off all salt. Pat dry.

Preheat oven to 350°F.

Spray large non-stick frying pan or saucepan; or lightly coat with oil. Melt margarine. Saute garlic and onion, partially covered, about 4 minutes over medium heat. Stir occasionally. Remove cover, add potatoes, and cook 2 minutes. Stir occasionally.

Spray a 2-quart ovenproof casserole, or lightly coat with oil. Spoon onion mixture into casserole. Add remaining vegetables, including eggplant, and stir to combine. Season with basil, oregano, salt, and pepper. Cover and bake on center rack of oven about 1 hour or until vegetables are tender. Remove cover after 30 minutes. Stir vegetables 3 or 4 times during baking.

Nutritional Data

PER SERVING		EXCHANGES	
Calories:	88	Milk:	0.0
Fat (gm):	0.5	Veg.:	1.0
Cholesterol (mg):	0	Fruit:	0.0
Sodium (mg):	233	Bread:	1.0
Potassium (mg):	643	Meat:	0.0
Sat. fat (gm):	0.1	Fat:	0.0
% Calories from fat:	5		

MOROCCAN CHICKEN OVER BAKED POTATOES

◆

Moroccan food boasts of many flavors blended together to a special spicy, tangy taste. If you like you can omit chicken and add cooked, chopped turnips or rutabagas for a vegetarian treat.
One teaspoon of freshly grated ginger root is equal to one-half teaspoon ginger powder. Ginger graters are sold at gourmet food shops and oriental markets.

◆

8 Servings

 4 baking potatoes, 5–6 ozs. each, skin on, scrubbed
Olive oil, or non-stick cooking spray
 1 chicken breast, about 8 ozs., skinned, boned, flattened slightly
 3 cloves garlic, minced
 1 cup onion, sliced
 1½ cups low-salt Chicken Stock (see Index)
 2 teaspoons cornstarch
 1 can, 16 ozs., crushed tomatoes, include liquid
 2 large tomatoes, peeled, chopped
 ¾ teaspoon turmeric
 ½ teaspoon, each ingredient: powdered ginger, ground cumin
 1 red or green bell pepper, sliced
 ⅛ teaspoon cayenne pepper
 ¼ cup green stuffed olives, sliced
 2 tablespoons pimiento, chopped
 ½ cup cilantro or parsley, minced

P reheat oven to 425°F. Scrub potatoes and stick several times with tip of sharp knife or fork. Set potatoes on non-stick cookie sheet. Bake on center rack of oven 45 minutes to 1 hour or until cooked. Potatoes are done when a knife inserted will test soft, or when squeezed gently will "give" slightly.

While potatoes are baking, prepare chicken and Moroccan sauce. Spray a non-stick frying pan; or lightly coat with oil. Saute chicken breast 2 to 4 minutes on each side over medium heat or until cooked through. Remove chicken to a plate and cut into ½-inch strips. Reserve.

Again spray frying pan. Saute garlic and onions, covered, over medium heat until onions are soft, stirring occasionally. Pour chicken stock into a bowl and whisk in cornstarch. Stir chicken stock into frying pan and add remaining ingredients. Add chicken. Simmer until hot, stirring occasionally.

Cut hot baked potatoes in half horizontally and gently squeeze open. Place potato halves on serving plate. Spoon chicken and sauce over potatoes. Serve hot.

Nutritional Data

PER SERVING		EXCHANGES	
Calories:	152	Milk:	0.0
Fat (gm):	1.9	Veg.:	1.0
Cholesterol (mg):	23	Fruit:	0.0
Sodium (mg):	145	Bread:	1.0
Potassium (mg):	570	Meat:	1.0
Sat. fat (gm):	0.4	Fat:	0.0
% Calories from fat:	11		

TURKEY CHILI BAKED POTATOES

Ground turkey is a substitute for the beef that is usually found in this recipe. Chili can be prepared ahead of time and frozen.
Most baking potatoes have a naturally elongated shape. Potatoes vary in shape, so pick your baking potatoes separately; do not buy them in a pre-mixed bag. Select the best-shaped potatoes and ones without blemishes.

8 Servings

- 4 baking potatoes, 5–6 ozs. each, skin on, scrubbed
  Canola oil, or non-stick cooking spray
- 4 cloves garlic, minced
- 1 cup onions, chopped
- ¾ lb. turkey, ground
- 1 can, 28 ozs., chopped tomatoes, include liquid
- 2 cans, 15½ ozs. each, kidney beans, include liquid from 1 can
- 3 tablespoons tomato paste
- 2 tablespoons chili powder
- ½ teaspoon oregano
- ¼ teaspoon pepper
- ⅛ teaspoon red pepper flakes

 reheat oven to 425°F. Scrub potatoes and stick several times, with tip of sharp knife or fork. Set potatoes on non-stick cookie sheet. Bake potatoes on center rack of oven 45 minutes to 1 hour or until cooked. Potatoes are done when a knife inserted will test soft, or when squeezed gently will "give" slightly.

While potatoes are baking, prepare chili. Spray a large, heavy saucepan; or lightly coat with oil. Saute garlic, onions, and ground turkey, covered, over medium heat. Cook until onions are soft, stirring occasionally. Mix in tomatoes and liquid, beans and liquid, and remaining ingredients. Bring mixture to boil, reduce heat to simmer, and continue cooking 30 minutes, stirring occasionally.

Cut hot baked potatoes in half horizontally and gently squeeze open. Place potatoes on serving dish, and spoon ¼ cup of chili over top of each. Serve hot. You might want to garnish each serving with 1 teaspoon of grated Cheddar cheese or a dollop of plain non-fat yogurt.

Nutritional Data

PER SERVING		EXCHANGES	
Calories:	256	Milk:	0.0
Fat (gm):	4	Veg.:	2.0
Cholesterol (mg):	16	Fruit:	0.0
Sodium (mg):	581	Bread:	2.0
Potassium (mg):	961	Meat:	1.0
Sat. fat (gm):	0.9	Fat:	0.0
% Calories from fat:	14		

BAKED POTATOES WITH PROVENÇAL VEGETABLES

Zucchini, eggplant, onions, and tomatoes are simmered to where all vegetables are melded together. This dish is even better if vegetables are prepared the day before serving.

8 Servings

- 4 baking potatoes, 5–6 ozs. each, skin on, scrubbed
- 1 small eggplant, about ¾ lb. cut into ½-in. rounds
  Olive oil, or non-stick cooking spray
- 4 cloves garlic, minced
- 2 medium zucchini, sliced
- 1 onion, sliced
- 1 green or red bell pepper, seeded, chopped
- 1 can, 16 ozs., crushed tomatoes, include liquid
- 1 teaspoon each ingredient: basil, tarragon, oregano
- ¼ teaspoon pepper, fresh-ground

 Preheat oven to 425°F. Scrub potatoes and stick several times with tip of sharp knife or fork. Set potatoes on non-stick cookie sheet. Bake on center rack of oven 45 minutes to 1 hour or until cooked. Potatoes are done when a knife inserted will test soft, or when squeezed will "give" slightly.

To prepare eggplant, sprinkle with salt, let stand 30 minutes over double layer of paper towels, drain under cold running water to remove salt, and pat dry.

While potatoes are baking, prepare vegetables. Spray a non-stick frying pan; or lightly coat with oil. Saute garlic and eggplant, covered, until eggplant is soft and golden brown. Cut eggplant into quarters; return it to pan. Add remaining ingredients. Simmer 20 minutes, stirring occasionally. Taste to adjust seasonings.

Cut hot baked potatoes in half horizontally and gently squeeze open. Place potato halves on serving dish. Spoon vegetables over potatoes and serve hot.

Nutritional Data

PER SERVING		EXCHANGES	
Calories:	111	Milk:	0.0
Fat (gm):	0.4	Veg.:	1.5
Cholesterol (mg):	0	Fruit:	0.0
Sodium (mg):	99	Bread:	1.0
Potassium (mg):	656	Meat:	0.0
Sat. fat (gm):	0.1	Fat:	0.0
% Calories from fat:	3		

Niçoise Salad over Baked Potatoes

Salad Niçoise is a combination of tuna, red onion, tomatoes, eggs (we use only the hard-cooked egg whites), fresh green beans, and, traditionally, small new potatoes. An olive oil and vinegar dressing is drizzled over the salad. Here we make the salad with the same wonderful combination of foods and serve it over a baked potato. The taste of the hot baked potato and cold salad is a good surprise.

---

8 Servings

4 baking potatoes, 5–6 ozs. each, skin on, scrubbed

1 can, 7 ozs., water-packed tuna, drained, mashed

2 cups fresh green beans, trimmed, cut into 1-in. pieces, cooked, drained

2 hard-boiled eggs, use only whites, chopped

1 medium red onion, chopped

2 cups tomatoes, chopped

2 anchovy filets, washed, patted dry, chopped

Dressing

2 tablespoons olive oil

1 tablespoon red wine vinegar

1 clove garlic, minced

½ teaspoon each ingredient: pepper, basil

 reheat oven to 425°F. Scrub potatoes and stick several times with tip of sharp knife or fork. Set potatoes on non-stick cookie sheet. Bake on center rack of oven 45 minutes to 1 hour or until potatoes are cooked. Potatoes are done when a knife inserted will test soft, or when squeezed gently will "give" slightly.

While potatoes are baking, prepare salad and dressing. Using a large mixing bowl, toss tuna with green beans, egg whites, onions, tomatoes, and anchovies. Set salad aside.

Dressing: In a small bowl, mix olive oil, red wine vinegar, garlic, pepper, and basil. Toss dressing with salad. Let stand 30 minutes. Toss salad before serving. (Salad can be prepared early in the day.)

When ready to serve, cut hot potatoes in half horizontally and gently squeeze open. Place potatoes on serving plate, and spoon salad over and around them.

Nutritional Data

PER SERVING		EXCHANGES	
Calories:	170	Milk:	0.0
Fat (gm):	4.4	Veg.:	2.0
Cholesterol (mg):	11	Fruit:	0.0
Sodium (mg):	157	Bread:	1.0
Potassium (mg):	614	Meat:	1.0
Sat. fat (gm):	0.7	Fat:	0.0
% Calories from fat:	23		

VEGETABLE FAJITAS

◆

Potatoes, onions, and peppers are the vegetables used in this dish. Together with flavorings, fajitas make an interesting meal with a Southwest flair.

8 Servings

Fajita Marinade

- ¼ cup canola oil
- 3 tablespoons lime juice, fresh-squeezed
- 1 teaspoon catsup
- ¼ teaspoon liquid mesquite smoke flavoring, optional
- ½ teaspoon garlic powder
- ¼ teaspoon each ingredient: ground cumin, ground chili powder

- 4 baking potatoes, 5–6 ozs. each, skin on, scrubbed

- 2 red bell peppers, cut into thin strips
- 1 large onion, sliced, separated into rings
  Canola oil, or non-stick cooking spray
- 1 all-purpose potato, about 6 ozs., peeled, cut into ½-in strips that resemble a French fry, cooked, drained
- 4 cloves garlic, minced

Fajita Marinade: In a bowl, mix oil, lime juice, catsup, liquid smoke, garlic powder, cumin, and chili powder. Pour marinade into large self-sealing plastic bag. Add bell peppers and onions. Seal bag securely and turn bag several times so all areas of vegetables are coated. Place bag in a flat dish and refrigerate 2 hours. Drain; reserve half of marinade.

Preheat oven to 425°F. About 1 hour before serving time, bake potatoes. Scrub potatoes and stick several times with tip of sharp knife or fork. Set potatoes on non-stick cookie sheet. Bake on center rack of oven 45 minutes to 1 hour or until cooked. Potatoes are done when a knife inserted will test soft, or when squeezed gently will "give" slightly.

Spray a large non-stick frying pan; or lightly coat with oil. Saute potato strips and garlic, covered, until potatoes begin to brown, stirring often, over medium heat. Add marinated bell peppers and onions, and continue cooking only until vegetables are hot but still crispy. Add 2 to 3 tablespoons of marinade as you cook.

Cut hot baked potatoes in half horizontally and gently squeeze open. Place potato halves on serving plate, and spoon vegetables over them. Serve hot.

Nutritional Data

PER SERVING		EXCHANGES	
Calories:	137	Milk:	0.0
Fat (gm):	3.6	Veg.:	0.5
Cholesterol (mg):	0	Fruit:	0.0
Sodium (mg):	10	Bread:	1.5
Potassium (mg):	456	Meat:	0.0
Sat. fat (gm):	0.3	Fat:	0.0
% Calories from fat:	23		

INDIAN CHICKPEAS AND TOMATOES OVER BAKED POTATOES

Baking potatoes are grown in many areas of the country, but the most famous are Idaho and Maine baking potatoes.
Chickpeas are dried peas that are available reconstituted in cans. This vegetable is important in Indian and Mediterranean cooking. They are also good in many salads and soups.

8 Servings

- 4 baking potatoes, 5–6 ozs. each, skin on, scrubbed
   Olive oil, or non-stick cooking spray
- 3 cloves garlic, minced
- 1 cup onions, chopped
- 1 can, 16 ozs., chickpeas
- 1 can, 16 ozs., chopped tomatoes, reserve liquid
- 2 tablespoons fresh lemon juice
- 2 tablespoons red wine vinegar
- ½ teaspoon each ingredient: ground cumin, curry powder
- ¼ teaspoon pepper

Preheat oven to 425°F. Scrub potatoes and stick with tip of sharp knife or fork several times. Set potatoes on non-stick cookie sheet. Bake on center rack of oven 45 minutes to 1 hour or until cooked. Potatoes are done when a knife inserted will test soft, or when squeezed gently will "give" slightly.

While potatoes are baking, prepare vegetables. Spray a non-stick frying pan; or lightly coat with oil. Saute garlic and onions, covered, until soft, stirring occasionally, over medium heat. Stir in remaining ingredients. Simmer and stir often until liquid is almost gone, about 10 minutes. Taste to adjust seasonings. Vegetables should be moist, not dry.

Cut hot baked potatoes in half horizontally and gently squeeze open. Place potato halves on serving plate and spoon vegetables over tops. Serve hot.

Nutritional Data

PER SERVING		EXCHANGES	
Calories:	94	Milk:	0.0
Fat (gm):	0.2	Veg.:	1.0
Cholesterol (mg):	0	Fruit:	0.0
Sodium (mg):	97	Bread:	1.0
Potassium (mg):	475	Meat:	0.0
Sat. fat (gm):	0.1	Fat:	0.0
% Calories from fat:	2		

CANTONESE STIR-FRY OVER BAKED POTATOES

8 Servings

- 4 baking potatoes, 5–6 ozs. each, skin on, scrubbed
  Canola oil, or non-stick cooking spray
- 2 cloves garlic, minced
- ½ teaspoon ginger root, fresh-grated
- 4 green onions, chopped
- ¾ lb. snow peas, trimmed
- 1 can, 6½ ozs., sliced water chestnuts, drained
- ½ cup carrots, grated
- 3 tablespoons dry white wine
- ½ cup low-salt Chicken Stock (see Index), mixed with 1 tablespoon cornstarch
- ¼ teaspoon pepper

P reheat oven to 425°F. Scrub potatoes and stick with tip of sharp knife or fork several times. Set potatoes on non-stick cookie sheet. Bake on center rack of oven 45 minutes to 1 hour or until potatoes are cooked. Potatoes are done when a knife inserted will test soft, or when squeezed gently will "give" slightly.

While potatoes are baking, prepare vegetables. Spray a non-stick wok or frying pan; or lightly coat with oil. Add garlic, ginger, and onions; stir-fry 1 minute over medium heat. Mix in snow peas, water chestnuts, and carrots. Stir-fry 2 minutes. Vegetables will be hot but not soggy. Sprinkle with wine, chicken stock mixture, and pepper. Cook only until mixture thickens slightly.

Cut hot baked potatoes in half horizontally and gently squeeze open. Spoon oriental stir-fry over potato halves. Serve hot.

Nutritional Data

PER SERVING		EXCHANGES	
Calories:	114	Milk:	0.0
Fat (gm):	0.2	Veg.:	2.0
Cholesterol (mg):	0	Fruit:	0.0
Sodium (mg):	10	Bread:	1.0
Potassium (mg):	472	Meat:	0.0
Sat. fat (gm):	0	Fat:	0.0
% Calories from fat:	2		

STIR-FRIED HOISIN VEGETABLES OVER BAKED POTATOES

Hoisin sauce is a bean-based oriental sauce. Many people prefer it to catsup. Dark, rich, and full bodied, just a small amount adds a lot of flavor to this dish. It is available at oriental food stores and many large supermarkets.

8 Servings

4 baking potatoes, 5–6 ozs. each, skin on, scrubbed

Canola oil, or non-stick cooking spray

2 cloves garlic, minced

½ teaspoon ginger root, fresh-grated

4 green onions, chopped

¾ lb. snow peas, trimmed

1 can, 6 ozs., sliced water chestnuts

½ cup carrot, grated

3 tablespoons dry white wine

2 tablespoons hoisin sauce

½ cup low-salt Chicken Stock (see Index)

1 tablespoon cornstarch

¼ teaspoon pepper

Preheat oven to 425°F. Scrub potatoes and stick several times with tip of sharp knife or fork. Set potatoes on non-stick cookie sheet. Bake on center rack of oven 45 minutes to 1 hour or until cooked. Potatoes are done when a knife inserted will test soft, or when squeezed gently will "give" slightly.

While potatoes are baking, prepare vegetables. Spray a non-stick wok or frying pan; or lightly coat with oil. Saute garlic, ginger, and onions 1 minute over medium-high heat. Stir as they cook. Mix in snow peas, water chestnuts, and carrots. Stir-fry 2 minutes. Vegetables should be hot but not soggy. Sprinkle with wine and hoisin sauce.

Pour chicken stock into bowl. Whisk in cornstarch and pepper. Mix stock mixture into stir-fry.

Cut hot baked potatoes in half horizontally and gently squeeze open. Place potato halves on serving plate, and spoon about ½ cup of stir-fry over each. Serve hot.

Nutritional Data

PER SERVING		EXCHANGES	
Calories:	154	Milk:	0.0
Fat (gm):	0.4	Veg.:	2.0
Cholesterol (mg):	0	Fruit:	0.0
Sodium (mg):	54	Bread:	1.5
Potassium (mg):	542	Meat:	0.0
Sat. fat (gm):	0.1	Fat:	0.0
% Calories from fat:	2		

SPANAKOPITA BAKED POTATOES

My son-in-law, from Greece, gave me the idea for this recipe. Spanakopita is a Greek spinach and ricotta cheese pie and one of Leo's favorite recipes.

8 Servings

4 baking potatoes, 5–6 ozs. each, skin on, scrubbed

Olive oil, or non-stick cooking spray

4 cloves garlic, minced

1 cup onions, chopped

3 cups fresh spinach, washed well, chopped

½ cup non-fat ricotta cheese

¼ teaspoon each ingredient: oregano, pepper, basil, ground nutmeg

 reheat oven to 425°F. Scrub potatoes and stick them several times with tip of sharp knife or fork. Set potatoes on non-stick cookie sheet. Bake on center rack of oven 45 minutes to 1 hour or until cooked. Potatoes are done when a knife inserted will test soft, or when squeezed gently will "give" slightly.

While potatoes are baking, prepare spinach topping. Spray a non-stick frying pan; or lightly coat with oil. Saute garlic and onions, covered, until onions are soft, stirring occasionally. Stir in spinach, cover, and continue cooking, stirring occasionally, until spinach is limp. Stir in cheese, oregano, pepper, basil, and nutmeg. Remove from heat.

Cut hot baked potatoes in half horizontally and gently squeeze open. Place potatoes on individual plates and spoon spinach filling over tops. Serve hot.

Nutritional Data

PER SERVING		EXCHANGES	
Calories:	97	Milk:	0.0
Fat (gm):	0.2	Veg.:	1.0
Cholesterol (mg):	1	Fruit:	0.0
Sodium (mg):	29	Bread:	1.0
Potassium (mg):	459	Meat:	0.0
Sat. fat (gm):	0	Fat:	0.0
% Calories from fat:	2		

MUSHROOMS AND CHEESE OVER BAKED POTATOES

Crimini mushrooms are a flavorful and heady-tasting vegetable. Criminis are also called Italian brown mushrooms. If they are not available in your area, substitute large white mushrooms.
Always use margarine that is cholesterol-free if you wish to keep personal levels down.

8 Servings

- 4 baking potatoes, 5–6 ozs. each, skin on, scrubbed
- 2 teaspoons margarine
- 2 cloves garlic, minced
- 4 shallots, minced
- 1 lb. fresh Crimini mushrooms, sliced
- ½ cup cholesterol-free cheese, grated

Preheat oven to 425°F. Scrub potatoes and stick with tip of sharp knife or fork several times. Set potatoes on non-stick cookie sheet. Bake on center rack of oven 45 minutes to 1 hour or until cooked. Potatoes are done when a knife inserted will test soft, or when squeezed gently will "give" slightly.

While potatoes are baking, prepare vegetables. Melt margarine in non-stick frying pan. Saute garlic and shallots 1 minute over medium heat, stirring occasionally. Add mushrooms and continue cooking, stirring occasionally, until mushrooms are done.

Cut hot baked potatoes in half horizontally and gently squeeze open. Place potato halves in a casserole, spoon mushrooms over them, and sprinkle with cheese. Bake potatoes in preheated 400°F. oven 5 minutes or until cheese is warm and has melted slightly.

Using a slotted spoon, remove potatoes to individual plates. Serve hot.

Nutritional Data

PER SERVING		EXCHANGES	
Calories:	113	Milk:	0.0
Fat (gm):	2.2	Veg.:	1.0
Cholesterol (mg):	0	Fruit:	0.0
Sodium (mg):	109	Bread:	1.0
Potassium (mg):	559	Meat:	0.0
Sat. fat (gm):	0.6	Fat:	0.5
% Calories from fat:	17		

CURRY JACKET POTATOES

◆

Jacket potatoes are the English version of our baked potatoes. The curry in this case is served over the baked potato and there are side dishes for toppings such as pineapple chunks, peanuts, chopped peppers, chopped green onions, cilantro, and chutney. We use all of the toppings except chutney. If you are determined to serve chutney, use only a small amount per person.
For a special treat, substitute baked sweet potatoes.

8 Servings

5 baking potatoes, 5–6 ozs. each, skin on, scrubbed
   Olive oil, or non-stick cooking spray
3 cloves garlic, minced
½ cup green onions, chopped
2 cups green or red bell peppers, sliced
2 cups cauliflower, cooked, drained, roughly chopped
2 cups Granny Smith apples, skin on, chopped
2 teaspoons curry powder
½ teaspoon ginger root, fresh-grated
¼ teaspoon each ingredient; pepper, ground cardamom
2 cups plain non-fat yogurt

Toppings
¼ cup chopped peanuts
½ cup chopped cilantro
½ cup chopped fresh pineapple
½ cup chopped hot (to taste) peppers
½ cup chopped green onions

 Preheat oven to 425°F. Scrub potatoes and stick several times with tip of sharp knife or fork. Set potatoes on non-stick cookie sheet. Bake on center rack of oven 45 minutes to 1 hour or until potatoes are cooked. Potatoes are done when a knife inserted will test soft, or when squeezed gently will "give" slightly.

While potatoes are baking, prepare vegetables and apples. Spray a non-stick frying pan; or lightly coat with oil. Saute garlic and onions, covered, over medium heat, stirring occasionally, until soft. Stir in vegetables, apples, and seasonings. Saute mixture over medium-low heat, covered, until just cooked, about 5 to 8 minutes. Remove from heat. Taste to adjust seasonings. Mix in yogurt.

Cut hot baked potatoes in half horizontally and gently squeeze open. Place potato halves on serving plate and spoon curry over them. Arrange toppings in small bowls for guests to help themselves.

Nutritional Data

PER SERVING		EXCHANGES	
Calories:	187	Milk:	0.5
Fat (gm):	2.7	Veg.:	0.0
Cholesterol (mg):	1	Fruit:	0.0
Sodium (mg):	179	Bread:	1.5
Potassium (mg):	771	Meat:	0.0
Sat. fat (gm):	0.4	Fat:	0.5
% Calories from fat:	13		

VEGETABLE CHILI OVER BAKED POTATOES

This recipe has all the advantages of chili flavoring and yet there is no beef. A variety of vegetables and beans are used instead of meat and beams, and then it is served over hot baked potatoes.

8 Servings

- 4 baking potatoes, 5–6 ozs. each, skin on, scrubbed
- 1 small eggplant, peeled, cut into slices. Olive oil, or non-stick cooking spray
- 3 cloves garlic, minced
- 1 cup green onions, chopped
- 1 cup green bell peppers, chopped
- 1 cup carrots, grated
- 2 cans, 15½ ozs. each, kidney beans, include liquid from 1 can
- 1 can, 28 ozs., chopped tomatoes, include liquid
- 3 tablespoons chili powder
- 2 tomatoes, chopped
- 2½ tablespoons chili powder
- ½ teaspoon each ingredient: oregano, ground cumin
- ¼ teaspoon pepper

reheat oven to 425°F. Scrub potatoes and stick several times with tip of sharp knife or fork. Set potatoes on non-stick cookie sheet. Bake on center rack of oven 45 minutes to 1 hour or until cooked. Potatoes are done when a knife inserted will test soft, or when squeezed gently will "give" slightly.

To prepare eggplant, sprinkle with salt and let stand 30 minutes on double layer of paper towels. Rinse under cold running water to remove salt and pat dry.

While potatoes are baking, prepare chili. Spray a large non-stick frying pan; or lightly coat with oil. Saute garlic and eggplant, covered, until eggplant is cooked, turning once. Eggplant is done when soft and golden brown. Chop.

Spray a large heavy saucepan with oil. Saute onions, peppers, and carrots, covered, about 5 minutes, stirring occasionally. Uncover and add remaining ingredients, including liquid from 1 can of beans. Bring mixture to boil; mix in eggplant. Reduce heat to simmer and continue cooking 20 minutes, stirring occasionally.

Cut hot baked potatoes in half horizontally and gently squeeze open. Place potato halves on serving plate, and spoon ¼ cup chili over each. Serve hot. You might want to garnish with chopped onions and or a dollop of plain non-fat yogurt.

Nutritional Data

PER SERVING		EXCHANGES	
Calories:	169	Milk:	0.0
Fat (gm):	0.8	Veg.:	2.0
Cholesterol (mg):	0	Fruit:	0.0
Sodium (mg):	349	Bread:	2.0
Potassium (mg):	909	Meat:	0.0
Sat. fat (gm):	0.1	Fat:	0.0
% Calories from fat:	4		

CHICKEN WITH STONE-GROUND MUSTARD OVER BAKED POTATOES

Vegetarians can simply substitute tofu for the chicken. Chill chicken breast for easy cutting.

8 Servings

4 baking potatoes, 5–6 ozs. each, skin on, scrubbed

Olive oil, or non-stick cooking spray

3 cloves garlic, minced

2 cups fresh green beans, trimmed, cut into 1-in. pieces

1 chicken breast, 6–8 ozs., skinned, boned, cubed

1¼ cups plain non-fat yogurt

1½ tablespoons stone-ground mustard

½ cup chives, chopped

½ teaspoon each ingredient; paprika, basil

 reheat oven to 425°F. Scrub potatoes and stick several times with tip of sharp knife or fork. Set potatoes on non-stick cookie sheet. Bake on center rack of oven 45 minutes to 1 hour or until potatoes are cooked. Potatoes are done when a knife inserted will test soft, or when squeezed gently will "give" slightly.

While potatoes are baking, prepare topping. Spray a non-stick frying pan; or lightly coat with oil. Saute garlic, green beans, and chicken over medium heat until chicken is just cooked through, stirring occasionally.

In small bowl, mix yogurt with mustard. Remove frying pan from heat. Stir in yogurt-mustard mixture.

Cut hot baked potatoes in half horizontally and gently squeeze open. Place potatoes on serving plate and spoon chicken with stone-ground mustard over top. Serve hot.

Nutritional Data

PER SERVING		EXCHANGES	
Calories:	139	Milk:	0.5
Fat (gm):	1	Veg.:	0.0
Cholesterol (mg):	18	Fruit:	0.0
Sodium (mg):	47	Bread:	1.0
Potassium (mg):	553	Meat:	0.5
Sat. fat (gm):	0.3	Fat:	0.0
% Calories from fat:	6		

CHICKEN FAJITAS OVER BAKED POTATOES

Baked potatoes with suitable toppings provide a complete meal. In England there are street vendors who sell "jacket" potatoes with various toppings to the fold passing by. They eat the hot potato right there on the street. It is very good.

8 Servings

Fajita Marinade

- ¼ cup canola oil
- 3 tablespoons lime juice, fresh-squeezed
- 1 teaspoon catsup
- 1 cup light beer
- ¼ teaspoon liquid smoke mesquite flavoring, optional
- ½ teaspoon garlic powder
- ¼ teaspoon each ingredient: ground cumin, ground chili powder

- 4 baking potatoes, 5–6 ozs. each, skin on, scrubbed

    Canola oil, or non-stick cooking spray
- 1 chicken breast, about 8 ozs., skinned, boned, cut into ½-in. strips
- 1 green bell pepper, cut into thin strips
- 1 red onion, sliced, separated into rings

 n a bowl, mix oil, lime juice, catsup, beer, liquid smoke, garlic powder, cumin, and chili powder. Pour marinade into large self-sealing plastic bag. Add chicken strips. Seal bag securely and turn several times so all areas of chicken are touched by marinade. Place bag in flat dish and refrigerate 2 hours. Drain; reserve 3 tablespoons marinade.

Preheat oven to 425°F. Scrub potatoes and stick several times with tip of sharp knife or fork. Set potatoes on non-stick cookie sheet. Bake on center rack of oven 45 minutes to 1 hour or until potatoes are cooked. Potatoes are done when a knife inserted will test soft, or when squeezed gently will "give" slightly.

Spray a large non-stick frying pan; or lightly coat with oil. Fry marinated chicken strips, pepper slices, and onion rings, covered, over medium heat until chicken is cooked through. Add 3 tablespoons of marinade to chicken and vegetables while they are cooking.

Cut hot baked potatoes in half horizontally and gently squeeze open. Place potato halves on serving plate and spoon the chicken fajita over them. Serve hot.

Nutritional Data

PER SERVING		EXCHANGES	
Calories:	141	Milk:	0.0
Fat (gm):	2.4	Veg.:	1.0
Cholesterol (mg):	23	Fruit:	0.0
Sodium (mg):	26	Bread:	1.0
Potassium (mg):	425	Meat:	1.0
Sat. fat (gm):	0.4	Fat:	0.0
% Calories from fat:	16		

SAUTEED ASPARAGUS AND MUSHROOMS OVER BAKED POTATOES

Potatoes can be baked successfully in the convection oven. The potatoes benefit from uniform temperature, which the convection oven achieves. Because of the design, little moisture escapes from the oven, which prevents the potatoes from drying out.

8 Servings

4 baking potatoes, 5–6 ozs. each, skin on, scrubbed

Olive oil, or non-stick cooking spray

3 shallots, minced

2 cups thin asparagus spears, cut into 2-in. pieces, blanched

1 lb. white mushrooms, or other mushrooms of your choice, trimmed, cleaned, sliced

2 tablespoons dry white wine

2 tablespoons parsley, minced

½ teaspoon basil

¼ teaspoon pepper

⅓ cup Parmesan cheese fresh-grated

P reheat oven to 425°F. Scrub potatoes and stick several times with tip of sharp knife or fork. Set potatoes on non-stick cookie sheet. Bake on center rack of oven 45 minutes to 1 hour or until cooked. Potatoes are done when a knife inserted will test soft, or when squeezed gently will "give" slightly.

While potatoes are baking, prepare vegetables. Spray a non-stick frying pan; or lightly coat with oil. Saute shallots 1 minute over medium heat. Add asparagus and mushrooms; cover. Continue cooking until mushrooms are cooked, about 5 minutes, stirring gently occasionally, not to break up asparagus. Sprinkle vegetables with wine as they cook. Stir in parsley, basil, and pepper. Cook until mushrooms are soft.

Cut hot baked potatoes in half horizontally and gently squeeze open. Place potato halves on serving plate. Divide vegetable mixture and spoon it onto potatoes. Sprinkle with freshly grated Parmesan cheese. Serve hot.

Nutritional Data

PER SERVING		EXCHANGES	
Calories:	120	Milk:	0.0
Fat (gm):	1.7	Veg.:	2.0
Cholesterol (mg):	3	Fruit:	0.0
Sodium (mg):	86	Bread:	1.0
Potassium (mg):	666	Meat:	0.0
Sat. fat (gm):	0.9	Fat:	0.0
% Calories from fat:	12		

6.
STEAMED POTATOES

in Black Bean Sauce

with Yogurt and Olives

with Orange Aroma

New Potatoes

Sweet Potatoes with Honey

with Tofu and Masala

with Fennel and Wine

Dressed New Potatoes

Oriental Steamed

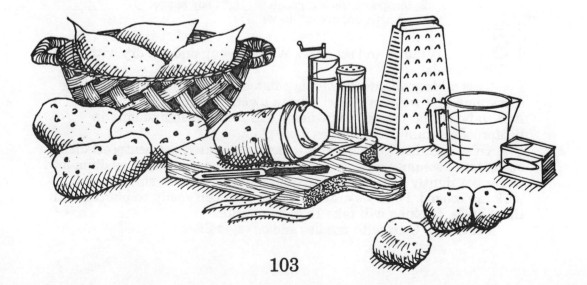

STEAMED POTATOES IN BLACK BEAN SAUCE

For steaming, use a steamer or improvise one, using a kettle, large pot, or wok. It must be large enough to accommodate a rack that will hold your food above the hot, steaming (but not boiling) water. A tight-fitting lid is most important. If you are not sure that the lid is tight fitting, cover the pot with a double layer of aluminum foil and set the cover on top of the foil. Steamed potatoes are done when they can be pierced easily with the tip of a sharp knife.

Oriental salted black beans are available at large supermarkets and at oriental food stores. Wash them well to remove all salt; mash them to use. The beans are available in small amounts.

8 Servings

16 new potatoes, scrubbed, peeled
¼ lb. large shrimp, shelled, deveined, cut in half lengthwise
3 ozs. leanest pork, such as tenderloin, ground
3 cloves garlic, minced
½ teaspoon powdered ginger
4 green onions, chopped
1 cup snow peas, trimmed
1 tablespoon salted black beans, soaked 5 minutes to remove salt, rinsed, mashed
¼ teaspoon sugar
2 teaspoons each ingredient: light soy sauce, cornstarch, dry white wine

Slice potatoes and set aside. Wash shrimp and pat dry with paper towels.

Toss all ingredients, including potatoes and shrimp but excluding cornstarch and wine, in a bowl. Whisk together cornstarch and wine. Add to bowl and toss all ingredients again. Place ingredients in heatproof steaming dish such as a pie plate.

Over high heat, bring water to boil in steamer. Set heatproof dish on center of steamer rack above water level. Reduce heat to medium-low. Cover pot tightly and continue steaming until potatoes, shrimp, and pork are cooked. Potatoes are done when they can easily be pierced with tip of knife. Cooking will take 15 to 20 minutes.

Serve hot. Good with noodles and/or vegetables.

Nutritional Data

PER SERVING		EXCHANGES	
Calories:	84	Milk:	0.0
Fat (gm):	0.6	Veg.:	0.0
Cholesterol (mg):	29	Fruit:	0.0
Sodium (mg):	80	Bread:	1.0
Potassium (mg):	299	Meat:	0.5
Sat. fat (gm):	0.2	Fat:	0.0
% Calories from fat:	6		

New Potatoes with Yogurt and Olives

Pick out well shaped, small potatoes for a pretty presentation. Either red or white new potatoes will be fine for this recipe. For special occasions, dab about ¼ to ½ teaspoon of whitefish roe on top of the yogurt. You can substitute ½ cup minced red onions for the olives

8 Servings

    Peel from 1 lemon
1½ lbs. new potatoes, skin on, scrubbed
1½ cups plain non-fat yogurt
  2 tablespoons green or black olives, minced

lace lemon peel in bottom of steamer. Add water and bring to boil over high heat. Position potatoes on steamer rack over hot water; cover. Reduce heat and continue cooking until potatoes are fork tender, 15 to 20 minutes, depending on thickness of potatoes.

While potatoes are cooking, spoon yogurt into small bowl. Mix in minced olives.

When potatoes are fork tender, using a slotted spoon, remove them to serving plate. Cut each potato in half. Using a small, sharp knife, trim bottom and top ends of potatoes so they will not roll when served.

Using a melon ball scoop or teaspoon, scoop out a small amount of potato from each half. Spoon yogurt onto potato and serve while hot.

Nutritional Data

PER SERVING		EXCHANGES	
Calories:	104	Milk:	0.5
Fat (gm):	0.3	Veg.:	0.0
Cholesterol (mg):	0	Fruit:	0.0
Sodium (mg):	42	Bread:	1.0
Potassium (mg):	441	Meat:	0.0
Sat. fat (gm):	0.1	Fat:	0.0
% Calories from fat:	3		

STEAMED POTATOES WITH ORANGE AROMA

By adding various items to the steaming water, you can infuse a subtle aromatic flavoring into the food. We use orange peel in this recipe, but you can use lemon peel or cinnamon.

8 Servings

Peel from 1 orange
4   boiling potatoes, 5–6 ozs. each, skin on, scrubbed
1   tablespoon orange peel, grated
1   cup breadcrumbs
½   cup carrots, grated
½   teaspoon oregano
¼   teaspoon garlic powder
⅛   teaspoon pepper

 rim orange peel, discarding excess pith. Add peel to water in bottom of steamer. Over high heat bring water to boil. Cut potatoes into quarters and position above the water in dish on steamer rack. Sprinkle potatoes with orange peel. Reduce heat to medium-low, cover pot tightly, and continue steaming until potatoes are tender, 15 to 20 minutes. Potatoes are done when they can easily be pierced by tip of a knife.

Prepare crumb topping by tossing remaining ingredients together in a bowl.

Remove steamer cover away from you to avoid hot steam; allow potatoes to cool slightly. Using slotted spoon, remove potatoes to cutting board. When cool enough to handle, slice potatoes. Put potatoes in a serving bowl and toss with crumb topping. Serve hot.

Nutritional Data

PER SERVING		EXCHANGES	
Calories:	90	Milk:	0.0
Fat (gm):	0.3	Veg.:	0.0
Cholesterol (mg):	0	Fruit:	0.0
Sodium (mg):	35	Bread:	1.5
Potassium (mg):	335	Meat:	0.0
Sat. fat (gm):	0.1	Fat:	0.0
% Calories from fat:	3		

STEAMED NEW POTATOES

This is one of those classic, wonderful yet simple recipes. Regardless of how you are preparing potatoes, always scrub them well under cold running water.

8 Servings

24 small new potatoes, scrubbed, peeled
2 sprigs dill, optional
2 tablespoons non-cholesterol margarine
⅛ teaspoon pepper
¼ cup fresh parsley or dill, minced

crub potatoes under cold running water. Add parsley or dill to water in bottom of steamer. Bring water to boil over high heat. Reduce heat to medium.

Position potatoes in dish on steamer rack. Water should be below rack. Cover pot tightly and continue steaming until potatoes are done, about 15 minutes. Potatoes are cooked when they can easily be pierced with tip of knife. Remove cover away from you to avoid hot steam.

Using a slotted spoon, place potatoes in serving bowl. Toss with margarine and pepper. Sprinkle fresh minced parsley or dill over potatoes. Serve hot. You might want to serve potatoes with plain non-fat yogurt or non-fat sour cream.

Nutritional Data

PER SERVING		EXCHANGES	
Calories:	79	Milk:	0.0
Fat (gm):	1.5	Veg.:	0.0
Cholesterol (mg):	0	Fruit:	0.0
Sodium (mg):	37	Bread:	1.0
Potassium (mg):	288	Meat:	0.0
Sat. fat (gm):	0.3	Fat:	0.0
% Calories from fat:	17		

STEAMED SWEET POTATOES WITH HONEY

♦

Just the slightest drizzle of honey on already sweet, sweet potatoes creates a holiday dish that you can serve anytime.

8 Servings

4 sweet potatoes, 5–6 ozs. each, peeled, cut into quarters
2 cups celery, chopped
Olive oil, or non-stick cooking spray
½ cup onions, chopped
3 large shallots, chopped
½ cup celery, chopped
½ teaspoon ground cinnamon
4 teaspoons honey

 Peel potatoes and cut into quarters. Bring water to boil over high heat in bottom of steamer. Place potatoes and 2 cups celery in heatproof dish and position on steamer rack. Water should be below rack. Reduce heat to medium-low. Cover pot tightly and continue steaming until potatoes can easily be pierced with tip of knife, 15 to 20 minutes. Remove cover away from you to avoid hot steam. While potatoes are cooking, prepare topping.

Spray a non-stick frying pan; or lightly coat with oil. Saute onions, shallots, and ½ cup celery, partially covered, until tender, about 4 minutes. Stir occasionally. Set aside.

With slotted spoon, remove potatoes and celery from steamer to deep bowl. Mash vegetables with cinnamon. Stir in sauteed vegetables. Spoon food into serving bowl and drizzle with honey.

♦

Nutritional Data

PER SERVING		EXCHANGES	
Calories:	96	Milk:	0.0
Fat (gm):	0.1	Veg.:	1.0
Cholesterol (mg):	0	Fruit:	0.0
Sodium (mg):	40	Bread:	1.0
Potassium (mg):	384	Meat:	0.0
Sat. fat (gm):	0	Fat:	0.0
% Calories from fat:	1		

STEAMED POTATOES AND TOFU WITH MASALA

Our masala is a combination of spices: cinnamon, cardamom, cumin, and cloves.

8 Servings

24 small new potatoes, scrubbed, peeled
1 package, 8 ozs., firm tofu, cut into ½-in. cubes
  Olive oil, or non-stick cooking spray
¾ cup onions, sliced
½ teaspoon ginger root, grated
3 cloves garlic, minced
¼ teaspoon each ingredient: turmeric, ground coriander, hot red pepper flakes
2 cups fresh or defrosted peas
3 tomatoes, chopped

Masala Mixture

½ teaspoon ground cinnamon
¼ teaspoon each ingredient: ground cardamom, ground cumin
⅛ teaspoon each ingredient: ground cloves, pepper

S crub potatoes. Fill steamer with enough water to come just below steamer rack. Bring water to boil. Reduce heat to medium. Position potatoes in heatproof dish on steamer rack, above hot water. Cover pot tightly and steam 10 minutes. Remove cover away from you to avoid steam and add tofu to steamer. Cover and continue steaming another 5 minutes or until potatoes are done and can easily be pierced with tip of knife. When potatoes are cool enough to handle, slice each into about 4 slices.

Spray a non-stick frying pan; or lightly coat with oil. Saute onion with ginger and garlic, partially covered, until tender. Stir occasionally. Mix in spices, masala mixture, potatoes, tofu, peas, and tomatoes. Partially cover and simmer 5 minutes, stirring occasionally. Taste to adjust seasonings. Serve hot.

Nutritional Data

PER SERVING		EXCHANGES	
Calories:	155	Milk:	0.0
Fat (gm):	2.8	Veg.:	1.0
Cholesterol (mg):	0	Fruit:	0.0
Sodium (mg):	47	Bread:	1.5
Potassium (mg):	542	Meat:	0.5
Sat. fat (gm):	0.4	Fat:	0.0
% Calories from fat:	16		

STEAMED NEW POTATOES AND FENNEL WITH WINE

The pink in the sauce is from the pink color of the zinfandel wine. It makes a very attractive presentation.

8 Servings

24 small new potatoes, scrubbed, peeled
2 fennel bulbs, trimmed, sliced
2 tablespoons parsley, minced
2 cloves garlic, minced
½ teaspoon fennel seeds

Pink Wine Sauce

1 tablespoon non-cholesterol margarine
1 tablespoon all-purpose flour
½ cup evaporated skim milk
½ cup pink zinfandel wine
⅛ teaspoon each ingredient: white pepper, fennel seeds

S crub potatoes under cold running water. Add enough water to steamer to reach just below steamer rack. Bring water to boil. Reduce heat to medium. Position potatoes and fennel in heatproof dish on steamer rack, above hot water. Sprinkle vegetables with parsley and garlic. Cover pot tightly and continue steaming until potatoes are done, about 15 minutes. Potatoes are cooked when they can easily be pierced with tip of knife. Remove cover away from you to avoid steam. When potatoes are cool enough to handle, remove vegetables to serving bowl, and drizzle with sauce. Serve hot.

Pink Wine Sauce: While vegetables are steaming, prepare sauce. Melt margarine in small, heavy saucepan over medium-low heat. Whisk in flour and continue cooking until flour is absorbed, 2 to 3 minutes. Whisk in evaporated skim milk and stir continuously until sauce thickens. Blend in wine and continue cooking, again, until sauce thickens slightly. Stir in pepper and fennel seeds.

Nutritional Data

PER SERVING		EXCHANGES	
Calories:	111	Milk:	0.5
Fat (gm):	1.4	Veg.:	0.0
Cholesterol (mg):	4	Fruit:	0.0
Sodium (mg):	59	Bread:	1.0
Potassium (mg):	360	Meat:	0.0
Sat. fat (gm):	0.8	Fat:	0.0
% Calories from fat:	12		

Dressed Steamed New Potatoes

The tart dressing over the hot steamed new potatoes makes an interesting, fast, elegant dish.

8 Servings

Red Wine Vinegar Dressing

2 tablespoons red wine vinegar
1 teaspoon olive oil
3 cloves garlic, minced
1 teaspoon honey mustard
1 cup tomatoes, chopped
½ cup celery, chopped
½ cup red onions, minced
¾ teaspoon basil
½ teaspoon marjoram
⅛ teaspoon pepper

24 new potatoes, scrubbed, peeled, cut in half

E arly in day, prepare sauce. In a bowl, whisk together vinegar, oil, garlic, and mustard. Toss tomatoes, celery, red onions, basil, marjoram, and pepper with dressing. Cover and refrigerate until serving time. Toss before serving.

Fill steamer with enough water to come just below steamer rack. Bring water to boil. Reduce heat to medium. Position potatoes in heatproof dish on steamer rack, above hot water. Cover pot tightly and continue steaming until potatoes are done, about 15 minutes. Potatoes are cooked when they can easily be pierced with tip of knife. Remove cover away from you to avoid steam. With slotted spoon remove potatoes to serving dish or bowl. Pour dressing over potatoes. Gently turn potatoes so that all surfaces are touched by dressing.

Nutritional Data

PER SERVING		EXCHANGES	
Calories:	84	Milk:	0.0
Fat (gm):	0.8	Veg.:	0.5
Cholesterol (mg):	0	Fruit:	0.0
Sodium (mg):	22	Bread:	1.0
Potassium (mg):	392	Meat:	0.0
Sat. fat (gm):	0.1	Fat:	0.0
% Calories from fat:	8		

ORIENTAL STEAMED POTATOES

The length of time it takes to steam potatoes depends on their thickness, that is, whether they are sliced or left whole. Also the amount of steam can vary depending on the amount of water, heat, or heat source. So times are approximate; test potatoes with the tip of a knife for doneness. Potatoes will pierce easily when done.
For aromatic infusion, you can add 1 chopped green onion to the steamer water and/or ½ teaspoon of ginger powder.

8 Servings

16 new potatoes, scrubbed, peeled
2 cups bok choy, sliced thin
1 cup spinach, washed well, trimmed
1 cup bamboo shoots, drained, sliced
4 green onions, chopped
½ teaspoon each ingredient: garlic powder, ginger powder
¼ teaspoon Chinese 5-spice powder
1 tablespoon cornstarch, mixed with 3 tablespoons low-salt Chicken Stock (see Index) or water

 lice each potato into about 4 slices and set aside. Toss bok choy, spinach, bamboo shoots, and onions in large bowl. Add garlic powder, ginger powder, and Chinese 5-spice powder. Toss ingredients. Add cornstarch mixture and toss once more.

Arrange seasoned vegetables and potatoes in heatproof steaming dish on steamer rack. Bring water to boil in bottom of steamer over high heat. Water should be below rack. Reduce heat to medium-low. Cover pot tightly and continue steaming until vegetables are cooked. Potatoes are done when they can easily be pierced with tip of knife, about 15 minutes. Remove cover away from you to avoid hot steam.

Serve hot.

Nutritional Data

PER SERVING		EXCHANGES	
Calories:	58	Milk:	0.0
Fat (gm):	0.1	Veg.:	0.5
Cholesterol (mg):	0	Fruit:	0.0
Sodium (mg):	14	Bread:	0.5
Potassium (mg):	366	Meat:	0.0
Sat. fat (gm):	0	Fat:	0.0
% Calories from fat:	2		

7.
POTATO SALADS

à la Caesar

Thai Potato and Chicken

Country with Mustard Dressing

Potato-Fish Salad

German

Potato, Green Bean, and Walnut

South American

Smoked Turkey

Grilled Sweet Potato

Potato-Cucumber

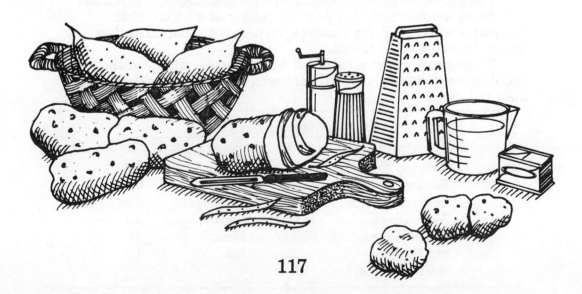

Potato Salad à la Caesar

With a few modifications, we have created a potato salad with Caesar-salad-like style. We use broken pieces of crisp romaine lettuce, a small amount of chopped anchovies, olives, and croutons. The raw egg white is eliminated from the dressing.

8 Servings

Dressing

- 3 tablespoons olive oil
- ½ teaspoon Worcestershire sauce
- 3 cloves garlic, minced
- ¼ teaspoon pepper
- 1 cup green onions, chopped
- 4 cups boiled new potatoes, skin on, cut in halves
- 6–8 cups romaine lettuce, torn into small bite-sized pieces
  Olive oil, or non-stick cooking spray
- 1 teaspoon non-cholesterol margarine
- 2 cloves garlic, minced
- ½ cup whole-wheat bread, crust removed, cubed for croutons
- 2 anchovies, washed, patted dry, minced
- 2 tablespoons ripe olives, sliced
- 2 tablespoons Parmesan cheese, fresh-grated

Dressing: In small bowl, whisk together oil, Worcestershire sauce, garlic, pepper, and onions.

Place potatoes in salad bowl. Toss with dressing. Mix in lettuce.

Spray a non-stick frying pan; or lightly coat with oil. Melt margarine with garlic. Fry croutons, turning with spatula as they brown. Drain on paper towels.

When ready to serve, top salad with croutons, minced anchovies, sliced olives, and freshly grated Parmesan cheese. Bring salad to table. Toss and serve.

Nutritional Data

PER SERVING		EXCHANGES	
Calories:	196	Milk:	0.0
Fat (gm):	6.4	Veg.:	0.0
Cholesterol (mg):	2	Fruit:	0.0
Sodium (mg):	111	Bread:	2.0
Potassium (mg):	686	Meat:	0.0
Sat. fat (gm):	1.1	Fat:	1.0
% Calories from fat:	29		

THAI POTATO AND CHICKEN SALAD

*It was not so long ago that cold pasta salad came into vogue. Well, why not potato salad.
You can use the same concept. Start with cooked, diced potatoes instead of pasta and add
various salad ingredients to make a complete meal and ready to serve.*

8 Servings

Salad

2½ cups boiled red potatoes, peeled, diced, skin on
1¾ cups cooked chicken, slivered
½ cup green onions, chopped
¾ cup carrots, grated
2 cups zucchini, sliced
½ cup sliced fruit such as apricots and bananas,
    sprinkled with lime juice
2 cups bean sprouts, washed, drained
2 tablespoons peanuts, chopped

Dressing

¼ cup orange juice, fresh-squeezed
2 teaspoons honey
2 tablespoons light soy sauce
2 tablespoons red wine vinegar
¼ teaspoon red pepper flakes
¼ teaspoon ground cumin

Salad: In a large mixing bowl, toss together all salad ingredients,
except bean sprouts and peanuts.

Dressing: Mix together all ingredients in small bowl. Toss salad
with dressing; taste to adjust seasonings.

Portion out salad on individual plates. Sprinkle with bean sprouts
and peanuts. Serve at room temperature.

Nutritional Data

PER SERVING		EXCHANGES	
Calories:	143	Milk:	0.0
Fat (gm):	1.8	Veg.:	2.0
Cholesterol (mg):	11	Fruit:	0.0
Sodium (mg):	159	Bread:	1.0
Potassium (mg):	583	Meat:	0.5
Sat. fat (gm):	0.3	Fat:	0.0
% Calories from fat:	11		

COUNTRY POTATO SALAD WITH MUSTARD DRESSING

Either for picnics or family fare, this stand-by is as good today as it was in our grandparents' time.

8 Servings

24 boiled new potatoes, about 1¼ lbs., skin on
4 hard boiled egg whites, chopped
1 cup celery, diced
1 cup sweet marinated peppers, chopped, drained (optional)
¼ cup plain non-fat yogurt
3 tablespoons cholesterol-free, reduced-calorie mayonnaise
2 teaspoons stone-ground mustard
½ teaspoon each ingredient: white pepper, garlic powder

Scrub potatoes. Put potatoes in saucepan and cover with water; bring to boil over medium-high heat. Reduce heat to medium and continue cooking until potatoes are fork tender, 15 to 20 minutes. Drain; pat dry and cool.

Slice or dice potatoes. Put potatoes into salad bowl and toss with egg whites, celery, and peppers.

In a small bowl, mix yogurt, mayonnaise, mustard, pepper, and garlic powder. Toss salad with dressing. Refrigerate salad before serving, or serve at room temperature.

Nutritional Data

PER SERVING		EXCHANGES	
Calories:	94	Milk:	0.0
Fat (gm):	2.1	Veg.:	0.0
Cholesterol (mg):	0	Fruit:	0.0
Sodium (mg):	95	Bread:	1.0
Potassium (mg):	348	Meat:	0.0
Sat. fat (gm):	0.4	Fat:	0.5
% Calories from fat:	20		

POTATO-FISH SALAD

Cooked fish has always blended well with cooked potatoes making an interesting and wholesome salad. For example, add to the salad a small amount of pickled herring, smoked fish, grilled fish, or almost any flavorful cooked fish. What a great use for leftover cooked fish. Bone the fish, cut or flake it, and add vegetables of your choice. The following recipe is good with grilled fish, pickled herring, or smoked fish.

8 Servings

2½ cups boiled potatoes, about 1½ lbs., skin on, diced

2 cups skinned, boned, cooked, grilled, or smoked fish, flaked

1 cup red onions, sliced

2 cups cherry tomatoes, cut in halves

2 cups lettuce, shredded

1 yellow or green bell pepper, seeded, chopped

3 tablespoons cilantro, minced, or fresh parsley

⅓–½ cup plain non-fat yogurt, or non-fat sour cream

1 tablespoon white horseradish, or to taste

 crub potatoes and quarter with skins on. To boil potatoes, cover with cold water in large saucepan. Bring water to boil over high heat. Reduce to medium heat and continue cooking, uncovered, until potatoes are fork tender, about 20 minutes. Drain, pat dry with paper towels, and dice when cool enough to handle. Put diced potatoes in large salad bowl.

If using herring, wash, pat dry, and cut into small pieces. Toss fish and vegetables with potatoes. Mix yogurt with horseradish for dressing and mix into salad. Refrigerate until serving time.

Nutritional Data

PER SERVING		EXCHANGES	
Calories:	130	Milk:	0.0
Fat (gm):	0.6	Veg.:	1.0
Cholesterol (mg):	21	Fruit:	0.0
Sodium (mg):	61	Bread:	1.0
Potassium (mg):	610	Meat:	0.5
Sat. fat (gm):	0.1	Fat:	0.0
% Calories from fat:	4		

GERMAN POTATO SALAD

New potatoes are usually cooked unpeeled for potato salads. More mature potatoes can be peeled or unpeeled and are sometimes used in these salads. The "new" potato is just what the name implies: a young potato.

8 Servings

- 1⅔ lbs. boiled small new or red potatoes, skin on
  Olive oil, or non-stick cooking spray
- ½ cup onions, chopped
- ⅓ cup low-salt Chicken or Vegetable Stock (see Index)
- ⅓ cup cider vinegar
- 2 teaspoons sugar
- ¾ teaspoon each ingredient: marjoram, celery seeds
- ¼ teaspoon each ingredient: salt, white pepper
- 2 tablespoons imitation bacon bits

 lace scrubbed new potatoes in saucepan and cover with water. Bring to boil over medium-high heat. Cook 15 to 20 minutes or until potatoes are just fork tender. Drain, pat dry, and cool.

Spray a non-stick frying pan; or lightly coat with oil. Saute onions, partially covered, over medium heat until tender. Stir occasionally. Stir in chicken stock, vinegar, sugar, marjoram, seeds, salt and pepper. Bring mixture to boil; cook 1 minute and remove from heat.

Cut potatoes in halves or slices; put in salad bowl. Toss with bacon bits. Add hot dressing and toss again. Serve hot or at room temperature.

Nutritional Data

PER SERVING		EXCHANGES	
Calories:	96	Milk:	0.0
Fat (gm):	0.5	Veg.:	1.0
Cholesterol (mg):	0	Fruit:	0.0
Sodium (mg):	112	Bread:	1.0
Potassium (mg):	385	Meat:	0.0
Sat. fat (gm):	0	Fat:	0.0
% Calories from fat:	4		

POTATO, GREEN BEAN, AND WALNUT SALAD

The small amount of walnuts adds a little crunch to the salad. You can substitute peanuts or pecans.

8 Servings

- 4 cups boiled red or new potatoes, skin on or peeled
- 1 lb. cooked green beans, trimmed, cut into 1½-in. pieces
- 1 can, 6½ ozs., sliced water chestnuts, drained
- 2 cups cherry tomatoes, cut in halves
- ¼ cup fat-free, cholesterol-free ranch dressing
- ½ teaspoon caraway seeds
- ⅓ cup walnuts, chopped

 lice potatoes. In a large serving bowl, toss potatoes with remaining ingredients, except walnuts.

Cover and chill until serving time. Toss salad gently and sprinkle with walnuts. Good for a large crowd. If serving salad individually, sprinkle walnuts equally on each portion.

Nutritional Data

PER SERVING		EXCHANGES	
Calories:	209	Milk:	0.0
Fat (gm):	3.4	Veg.:	2.0
Cholesterol (mg):	0	Fruit:	0.0
Sodium (mg):	64	Bread:	2.0
Potassium (mg):	989	Meat:	0.0
Sat. fat (gm):	0.3	Fat:	0.5
% Calories from fat:	14		

SOUTH AMERICAN POTATO SALAD

Peru is home to the potato. So it is natural that we should have a recipe from south of the border.
An interesting note about microwaving is that a whole potato cooks faster than sliced potatoes because the skin helps hold in the heat.

8 Servings

- 8 boiled red or new potatoes, 5–6 ozs. each, skin on or peeled
- 2 cups pot cheese, or small-curd cottage cheese
- ½ teaspoon each ingredient: salt, pepper, chili powder, turmeric, garlic powder
- ¼ cup skim milk
- 2 tablespoons olive oil
- ½ cup green onions, minced
- 3 hard boiled egg whites, chopped
- ¼ cup cilantro, minced

 ut potatoes in half; place in saucepan. Cover potatoes with water. Bring to boil over medium-high heat. Cook 15 to 20 minutes or until potatoes are just fork tender. Drain, cool, and slice potatoes. Transfer potatoes to salad bowl.

Using a blender or food processor fitted with steel blade, puree cheese with seasonings, milk, and oil.

Toss potatoes with dressing. Sprinkle salad with onions, chopped egg whites, and cilantro.

Nutritional Data

PER SERVING		EXCHANGES	
Calories:	237	Milk:	0.0
Fat (gm):	4.7	Veg.:	0.0
Cholesterol (mg):	5	Fruit:	0.0
Sodium (mg):	396	Bread:	2.0
Potassium (mg):	718	Meat:	1.0
Sat. fat (gm):	1.2	Fat:	1.0
% Calories from fat:	18		

SMOKED TURKEY POTATO SALAD

As with so many recipes at home, when we smoked a turkey, there were lots of leftovers. So the marriage of smoked turkey and potato quickly came to be in the form of a salad. You can substitute cooked chicken or tofu for the smoked turkey.

8 Servings

2½ cups boiled red or new potatoes, skin on or peeled

Olive oil, or non-stick cooking spray

1 tablespoon non-cholesterol margarine

1½–2 cups smoked skinless white turkey meat, cubed or shredded

2 cups celery, chopped

¼ cup dried onion flakes

½ cup parsley, chopped

3 hard boiled egg whites, chopped

½ teaspoon each ingredient: basil, paprika

¼ teaspoon each ingredient: salt, pepper

3 tablespoons cholesterol-free, reduced-calorie mayonnaise

¼ cup plain non-fat yogurt

 lice potatoes. Spray a non-stick frying pan; or lightly coat with oil. Melt margarine over medium heat. Fry potatoes, stirring as they turn a golden brown, 3 to 5 minutes. Potatoes will break up into pieces. Set aside.

In a large serving bowl, toss turkey, potatoes, and remaining ingredients, except mayonnaise and yogurt. In a small bowl, mix mayonnaise and yogurt for dressing. Toss salad with dressing.

Serve cold or at room temperature on a bed of lettuce.

Nutritional Data

PER SERVING		EXCHANGES	
Calories:	151	Milk:	0.0
Fat (gm):	2.9	Veg.:	1.0
Cholesterol (mg):	18	Fruit:	0.0
Sodium (mg):	182	Bread:	1.0
Potassium (mg):	529	Meat:	1.0
Sat. fat (gm):	0.6	Fat:	0.0
% Calories from fat:	17		

GRILLED SWEET POTATO SALAD

To bake sweet or white potatoes in the microwave, first pierce potato several times; bake on High. A single medium-size potato bakes in 7 to 9 minutes. Let potato stand 2 minutes before serving. You can turn potato over once during baking.

4 Servings

2 medium sweet potatoes, 5–6 ozs. each, scrubbed
1 lb. asparagus, trimmed
2 oranges, peeled, cut into ¼–½-in. slices
Non-stick cooking spray
4 cups lettuce, sliced, washed, spun dry

Brushing Sauce
⅓ cup sweet and spicy fat-free salad dressing
¼ teaspoon curry powder

Spiced Mayonnaise
3 tablespoons cholesterol-free, reduced-calorie mayonnaise
¼ teaspoon each ingredient: curry powder, ground cinnamon

Peel potatoes and cut in halves. Put potatoes in saucepan, cover with cold water, and boil over medium-high heat until just about cooked. Drain. When potatoes are cool enough to handle, cut into ¼ to ½-inch slices.

Trim asparagus, discarding woody stems. Boil until just about cooked, leaving asparagus slightly crisp. Drain.

Brushing Sauce: Mix together salad dressing and curry powder.

Spiced Mayonnaise: Mix together mayonnaise and spices.

When coals are hot, position a sprayed grill screen on barbecue. If you have a small grill, it might be necessary to grill the food in batches. Position sweet potatoes, asparagus, and oranges on grill screen, and brush with brushing sauce as you grill. Turn potatoes, asparagus, and orange slices as necessary until they are hot and charred slightly on both sides.

Arrange lettuce on individual dishes. Using a long-handled spatula, remove vegetables and oranges and arrange decoratively over lettuce. Spoon a dollop of spiced mayonnaise in center of each salad. Serve hot.

Nutritional Data

PER SERVING		EXCHANGES	
Calories:	201	Milk:	0.0
Fat (gm):	4.7	Veg.:	1.0
Cholesterol (mg):	0	Fruit:	1.0
Sodium (mg):	166	Bread:	1.0
Potassium (mg):	781	Meat:	0.0
Sat. fat (gm):	0.9	Fat:	1.0
% Calories from fat:	20		

POTATO-CUCUMBER SALAD

A light refreshing salad, try this for a picnic. To seed the cucumber, slice it in half lengthwise and with a spoon, scoop out and discard seeds.

8 Servings

2½ cups boiled red or new potatoes, about
    1½ lbs., skin on
    Olive oil, or non-stick cooking spray
1   tablespoon non-cholesterol margarine
2   cloves garlic, minced
1   cup onions, sliced
1   large cucumber, seeded, sliced thin
2   cups plain non-fat yogurt, or cottage cheese
1   tablespoon each ingredient: red wine vinegar,
    basil
2   tablespoons fresh dill, chopped
¼   teaspoon white pepper

P lace diced potatoes in saucepan; cover with water. (If potatoes are to stand for any length of time, place them in a glass bowl and cover with cold water. Drain well and pat dry with paper towels before using.) Bring potatoes to boil over medium-high heat. Reduce heat to medium and cook about 8 minutes or until potatoes are just fork tender. Drain.

Spray a non-stick or regular wok or frying pan; or lightly coat with oil. Melt margarine. Stir-fry garlic and onions, covered, over medium-high heat 4 minutes. Stir occasionally. Add potatoes and cook until brown, stirring occasionally. Spoon vegetables into salad bowl; cool.

Mix in cucumber, yogurt, red wine vinegar, basil, dill, and white pepper. Toss salad with dressing. If you are not going to use salad immediately, cover and refrigerate until needed. Toss salad again before serving.

Nutritional Data

PER SERVING		EXCHANGES	
Calories:	126	Milk:	0.5
Fat (gm):	1.0	Veg.:	0.5
Cholesterol (mg):	1	Fruit:	0.0
Sodium (mg):	65	Bread:	1.0
Potassium (mg):	563	Meat:	0.0
Sat. fat (gm):	0.2	Fat:	0.0
% Calories from fat:	7		

8.
POTATOES ON THE GRILL

Baked Potatoes

New Potatoes with Chili Sauce

Tandoori-Flavored Vegetable Kabobs

Tandoori Chicken and Potato Kabobs

Double-Baked with Basil Sauce

Teriyaki with Pea Pods and Mushrooms

Sweets with Peppers and Tomatoes

Grilled with Vegetables and Pasta

Grilled with Red Onions

Broccoli and Potato Kabobs with Chili Sauce

Grilled Skins with Salsa

New Potato, Artichoke, and Red Onion Kabobs

Grilled Sweets with Pineapple

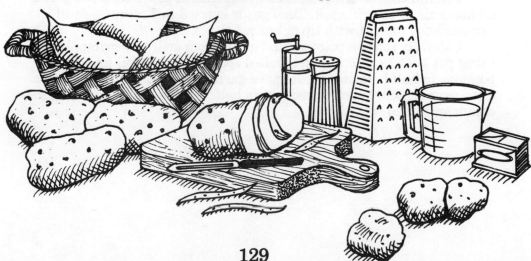

129

BAKED POTATOES ON THE GRILL

In the technique of grilling, you position food on the grill rack 5 to 6 inches above the hot coals. This dry heat method allows the food to take on the smoky flavors of the charcoal. For best results, use hardwood charcoal along with aromatic wood, which can be obtained locally or from Peoples Smoke and Grill, 75 Mill St., Cumberland, RI 02864 (1-800-729-5800). In this recipe we grill potatoes and garlic directly over the coals. Garlic takes on a less pungent taste when baked and is easy to squeeze out of the skin, which can be discarded.

8 Servings

4   baking potatoes, 5–6 ozs. each, skin on,
    scrubbed
4   large cloves garlic, skin intact
    Aluminum foil, heavy-duty
4   tablespoons cholesterol-free, non-fat sour
    cream, or plain non-fat yogurt
½   cup chives, chopped

crub potatoes under cold running water. Separately wrap potatoes and garlic cloves in heavy-duty aluminum foil. Remove grill rack and set potatoes directly on hot coals, around perimeter of barbecue grill. If you are grilling other food at this time, replace grill rack and cook as directed. Potatoes should be turned every 10 minutes until done. Potatoes are cooked when easily pierced with tip of knife, 35 to 40 minutes, depending on size of potato, heat, and outdoor temperature.

Ten minutes before estimated finish time of potatoes, place garlic on hot coals or on grill rack. Turn garlic every 3 to 8 minutes until it can easily be pierced with tip of knife.

Carefully remove potatoes and garlic from grill to serving plate, using pot holders and/or long-handled spoon. Remove foil and cut potatoes in half horizontally. Remove garlic from foil. Squeeze a garlic clove over center of each baked potato half. Serve hot with dollop of sour cream sprinkled with chives.

Nutritional Data

PER SERVING		EXCHANGES	
Calories:	90	Milk:	0.0
Fat (gm):	0.1	Veg.:	0.5
Cholesterol (mg):	0	Fruit:	0.0
Sodium (mg):	24	Bread:	1.0
Potassium (mg):	318	Meat:	0.0
Sat. fat (gm):	0	Fat:	0.0
% Calories from fat:	1		

NEW POTATOES WITH HOMEMADE CHILI SAUCE

Make extra chili sauce to give as gifts. If storing it, follow jar manufacturer's directions for preserving. This recipe can easily be doubled.

4 Servings

Chili Sauce

- 2 cups ripe tomatoes, chopped
- ¼ cup each ingredient: chopped onion, chopped green pepper
- 2 teaspoons sugar
- ½ teaspoon ginger root, fresh-grated
- ½ teaspoon ground cinnamon
- ¼ teaspoon salt
- ⅛ teaspoon nutmeg, fresh-grated
- ¼ cup red wine vinegar

- 8 new potatoes, skin on
- 1 large red bell pepper, seeded, cut into 1-in. pieces
- 4 green onions, trimmed, cut into 3-in. lengths
- 4 small double-pronged skewers, or bamboo skewers soaked in water 15 minutes and drained
  Canola oil, or non-stick cooking spray

Chili Sauce: Mix all ingredients, except vinegar, together in heavy saucepan. Bring sauce to boil; reduce heat to simmer. Simmer until mixture thickens, about 10 minutes, stirring occasionally. Stir in vinegar. Taste to adjust seasonings. Cool. Place in covered bowl and refrigerate until serving time.

Scrub potatoes under cold running water. Parboil potatoes in water until just fork tender. Drain. When potatoes are cool enough to handle, cut into halves.

Thread skewers, alternating peppers, onions, and potatoes. Add extra peppers and onions at end of skewers. Brush vegetables lightly with about 1 teaspoon of chili sauce.

When coals are hot, position a sprayed grill screen on grill. Place skewers on screen. Grill kabobs, turning frequently and brushing with additional teaspoons of chili sauce.

To serve, set a kabob on each plate and pass extra chili sauce at the table.

Nutritional Data

PER SERVING		EXCHANGES	
Calories:	86	Milk:	0.0
Fat (gm):	0.5	Veg.:	2.0
Cholesterol (mg):	0	Fruit:	0.0
Sodium (mg):	146	Bread:	0.5
Potassium (mg):	508	Meat:	0.0
Sat. fat (gm):	0.1	Fat:	0.0
% Calories from fat:	5		

TANDOORI-FLAVORED VEGETABLE KABOBS

Tandoori refers to an Indian cooking method. The tandoor is a large clay oven, which rises to high heat, using charcoal. Its roots may be in ancient Persia. Many Indian restaurants have a tandoor oven. To simulate this method at home, we can use the outdoor barbecue grill.

8 Servings

Tandoori Marinade
- 1 cup plain non-fat yogurt
- 1 tablespoon red wine vinegar
- ½ teaspoon each ingredient: dry mustard, ground cumin
- ¼ teaspoon each ingredient: red pepper flakes, ground ginger, ground turmeric
- 2 cloves garlic, minced

- 2 boiled red or new potatoes, 5–6 ozs. each, skin on, cut into ¾-in slices
- 1 large onion, cut in half, rings separated
- 2 zucchini, cut into 1½-in. pieces, cooked, drained
- 1 red bell pepper, cut into 2-in. pieces
- 8 double-pronged or bamboo skewers
  Non-stick cooking spray

Tandoori Marinade: In a glass bowl, mix yogurt, vinegar, spices, and garlic. Toss vegetables in marinade and let stand 1 hour.

Thread skewers, alternating among potato slices, onions, zucchini, and pepper pieces.

Preheat outdoor grill until coals are glowing. Spray grill screen or rack and position it about 6 inches from heat source. Put kabobs on grill and cook, turning as vegetables begin to char. Kabobs are done when vegetables are hot and browned slightly. To serve, place skewers on individual plates or on serving platter.

Nutritional Data

PER SERVING		EXCHANGES	
Calories:	61	Milk:	0.0
Fat (gm):	0.2	Veg.:	1.0
Cholesterol (mg):	0	Fruit:	0.0
Sodium (mg):	25	Bread:	0.5
Potassium (mg):	332	Meat:	0.0
Sat. fat (gm):	0	Fat:	0.0
% Calories from fat:	3		

TANDOORI CHICKEN AND POTATO KABOBS

It is the interesting Indian combination of spices that makes these kabob so good.

8 Servings

Tandoori Marinade

- 1½ cups plain non-fat yogurt
- 1½ tablespoons cider vinegar
- ½ teaspoon each ingredient: dry mustard, ground cumin
- ¼ teaspoon each ingredient: grated ginger, red pepper flakes, ground ginger, ground turmeric
- 3 cloves garlic, minced

- 1 chicken breast, 8–10 ozs., skinned, boned, flattened, cut into ¾-in. strips
- 16 new potatoes, parboiled, skin on, until just fork tender, drained
- 8 green onions, cut into 2-in. pieces
- 1 cucumber, peeled, cut into thin slices
- 8 double-pronged or bamboo skewers
  Non-stick cooking spray

Tandoori Marinade: In a glass bowl, mix yogurt, vinegar, spices, and garlic. Toss chicken and vegetables in marinade and let stand 1 hour.

Thread skewers with chicken strips, potatoes, green onions, and cucumbers.

Preheat outdoor grill until coals are glowing. Spray grill screen or rack and position it about 6 inches from heat source. Put kabobs on grill and cook, turning as vegetables begin to char. Kabobs are done when chicken is cooked through and vegetables are hot and browned slightly. To serve, place skewers on individual plates or on serving platter.

Nutritional Data

PER SERVING		EXCHANGES	
Calories:	106	Milk:	0.0
Fat (gm):	1	Veg.:	0.0
Cholesterol (mg):	19	Fruit:	0.0
Sodium (mg):	51	Bread:	1.0
Potassium (mg):	421	Meat:	1.0
Sat. fat (gm):	0.3	Fat:	0.0
% Calories from fat:	8		

DOUBLE-BAKED POTATOES WITH BASIL SAUCE

8 Servings

4 baking potatoes, 5–6 ozs. each, skin on, scrubbed
Aluminum foil, heavy-duty

Basil Sauce

½ cup basil leaves, cleaned, firmly packed
2 cloves garlic
¼ teaspoon powdered ginger
¼ cup fresh parsley, or spinach, chopped
1 cup plain non-fat yogurt
¼ teaspoon each ingredient: salt, white pepper

S crub potatoes under cold running water. Individually wrap potatoes in heavy-duty aluminum foil. When coals are hot, remove grill rack and set potatoes directly on hot coals around perimeter of barbecue grill. If you are grilling other food at this time, replace grill rack and cook as directed. Potatoes should be turned every 10 minutes until done. Potatoes are cooked when easily pierced with tip of knife, 35 to 40 minutes, depending on size of potato, heat, and outdoor temperature.

Basil Sauce: While potatoes are "grilling," prepare sauce. Puree all sauce ingredients in blender or food processor fitted with steel blade. Spoon sauce into bowl, cover, and refrigerate until serving time.

Carefully remove potatoes from grill to kitchen counter, using pot holders and/or long-handled spoon. Discard foil. Cut potatoes in halves horizontally. With a spoon, scoop out potato meat, leaving skin intact with small lining of potato. While potatoes are still hot, mash scooped out meat and mound it back into potato skins.

Place potatoes back on grill rack or grill screen, cover, and grill 5 minutes more until potatoes are hot.

Using pot holders or long handled spoon, remove potatoes to individual plates. Spoon basil sauce over potatoes. Serve hot.

Nutritional Data

PER SERVING		EXCHANGES	
Calories:	90	Milk:	0.0
Fat (gm):	0.2	Veg.:	0.5
Cholesterol (mg):	0	Fruit:	0.0
Sodium (mg):	95	Bread:	1.0
Potassium (mg):	409	Meat:	0.0
Sat. fat (gm):	0.1	Fat:	0.0
% Calories from fat:	2		

POTATOES TERIYAKI WITH PEA PODS AND MUSHROOMS

Kabobs are a natural cooking method for potatoes because of the tuber's shape and the ease in cutting it to a perfect size for grilling. The potato is partially cooked before threading onto skewers. Grilling gives potatoes an interesting smoky flavor, and when combined with brushing sauce, you have a good-tasting appetizer, side dish, or complete meal. If you use bamboo skewers, soak them in water 15 minutes before using.

8 Servings

- 8   short double-pronged or bamboo skewers
- 24 snow peas, trimmed
- 16 new potatoes, skin on, scrubbed and parboiled until just fork tender, drained
- ¼   lb. fresh shiitaki mushrooms, trimmed

Brushing Sauce

- ¼   cup low-salt Chicken Stock (see Index)
- 1   tablespoon light soy sauce
- 2   tablespoons dry white wine
- ¼   teaspoon garlic powder
- ½   teaspoon sugar

Thread skewers, alternating snow peas, new potatoes, and shiitaki mushrooms.

Brushing Sauce: Combine all ingredients in small bowl. Brush kabobs with sauce.

Preheat outdoor grill until coals are glowing. Spray grill screen or rack and position it about 6 inches above heat source. Place kabobs on grill and cook, turning as vegetables begin to char. Kabobs are done when vegetables are hot and browned. To serve, place skewers on individual plates and serve hot.

Nutritional Data

PER SERVING		EXCHANGES	
Calories:	61	Milk:	0.0
Fat (gm):	0.1	Veg.:	0.0
Cholesterol (mg):	0	Fruit:	0.0
Sodium (mg):	91	Bread:	1.0
Potassium (mg):	218	Meat:	0.0
Sat. fat (gm):	0	Fat:	0.0
% Calories from fat:	2		

SWEET POTATOES WITH PEPPERS AND TOMATOES

This sweet potato kabob makes a pretty presentation as a vegetable or side dish. If you are grilling anyway, it isn't much bother to grill the vegetables also. This dish is good with fish or by itself.

8 Servings

- 4 short double-pronged skewers, or regular skewers
- 2 sweet potatoes, 5–7 ozs. each, peeled
- 8 banana peppers, or 2 bell peppers, cut in half horizontally, seeded
- 16 cherry tomatoes, washed, stems removed

Brushing Sauce

- 2 teaspoons non-cholesterol margarine, melted
- ¼ teaspoon each ingredient: ground cumin, ground cinnamon
- ¼ cup cilantro, minced, or chives, minced
  Non-stick cooking spray

ut potatoes into 1½-inch chunks and parboil until just fork tender; drain.

Thread skewers, alternating sweet potatoes, peppers, and cherry tomatoes.

Brushing Sauce: Mix melted margarine with ground cumin, cinnamon and cilantro. Lightly brush kabobs with brushing sauce.

Preheat outdoor grill or use a Burton stove-top grill; make sure that you follow manufacturer's directions. Spray grill rack. Position kabobs over hot, glowing coals about 6 inches from heat. Cook, turning kabobs as vegetables begin to char. Kabobs are done when vegetables are hot and browned.

To serve, place skewers on individual plates and serve hot.

Nutritional Data

PER SERVING		EXCHANGES	
Calories:	71	Milk:	0.0
Fat (gm):	0.9	Veg.:	1.5
Cholesterol (mg):	0	Fruit:	0.0
Sodium (mg):	23	Bread:	0.5
Potassium (mg):	257	Meat:	0.0
Sat. fat (gm):	0.1	Fat:	0.0
% Calories from fat:	10		

GRILLED POTATOES AND VEGETABLES WITH PASTA

*The vegetables can be served alone, as a side dish, or as a complete vegetarian **meal**. This recipe call for tossing them with spinach pasta for a salad.*

4 Servings

- 2 boiling potatoes, 5–6 ozs. each, skin on
- 1 small eggplant, peeled, sprinkled with salt, placed on double layer of paper towels for 15 minutes
- 1 bunch green onions
- 2 firm tomatoes
  Non-stick cooking spray

Basil Red Sauce

- Olive oil, or non-stick cooking spray
- 1 cup onions, chopped
- 3 cloves garlic, minced
- ½ cup carrots, shredded
- 1 can, 16 ozs., crushed tomatoes, include juice
- ¾ teaspoon basil
- ¼ teaspoon pepper
- 1 tablespoon black olives, chopped

- 2 cups spinach pasta, cooked, drained

 crub potatoes under cold running water. Parboil potatoes until just fork tender. Drain. When potatoes are cool enough to handle, cut into thin slices. Set aside.

Wash salt off eggplant and pat dry with paper towels. Trim green onions; leave whole.

Basic Red Sauce: Spray or lightly oil a non-stick pan. Saute chopped onions and garlic, partially covered, until onions are soft, stirring occasionally. Add remaining ingredients. Simmer sauce 5 minutes, stirring occasionally. Set aside.

When coals are hot, position sprayed grill screen or rack on grill. Set vegetables, except tomato slices, on grill. Cook vegetables, turning and brushing lightly with basil red sauce as you turn. Vegetables will get hot and char slightly. Add tomatoes just before vegetables are done, brushing with sauce, and grilling 1 minute on each side.

Remove vegetables with long-handled spatula to bowl. Cut eggplant and tomatoes into quarters. Toss potatoes, eggplant, and tomatoes with pasta. Divide onto individual dishes. Spoon 2 tablespoons of sauce on top of each portion. Place grilled green onions on the side. Serve hot. You may want to top with freshly grated Parmesan cheese.

Nutritional Data

PER SERVING		EXCHANGES	
Calories:	233	Milk:	0.0
Fat (gm):	2.2	Veg.:	3.0
Cholesterol (mg):	19	Fruit:	0.0
Sodium (mg):	276	Bread:	2.0
Potassium (mg):	1086	Meat:	0.0
Sat. fat (gm):	0.4	Fat:	0.0
% Calories from fat:	8		

GRILLED NEW POTATOES WITH RED ONIONS

If new potatoes are not available, quarter four, 5-to-6-ounce white or red potatoes.

---

8 Servings

- 16 medium new potatoes, skin on
- 2 medium red onions, cut into ½-in. slices
- ¼ cup non-fat Italian salad dressing
  Non-stick cooking spray
- 2 tablespoons plus ½ teaspoon rosemary, rinsed, drained

 Scrub potatoes under cold running water. Cook potatoes until almost done. Drain. When potatoes are cool enough to handle, cut into ½-inch slices. Brush both potatoes and onion slices with Italian salad dressing.

Spray grill screen and set on grill. Sprinkle 2 tablespoons rosemary on hot coals. When coals are hot, position potato and onion slices on screen. Sprinkle with ½ teaspoon rosemary. Cook until vegetables are just charred and hot. Turn frequently, as necessary. Brush vegetables with dressing as they cook or as you turn them.

Using a long-handled spatula, remove vegetables to serving bowl; bring to table hot.

Nutritional Data

PER SERVING		EXCHANGES	
Calories:	58	Milk:	0.0
Fat (gm):	0.1	Veg.:	0.0
Cholesterol (mg):	0	Fruit:	0.0
Sodium (mg):	19	Bread:	1.0
Potassium (mg):	240	Meat:	0.0
Sat. fat (gm):	0	Fat:	0.0
% Calories from fat:	2		

BROCCOLI AND NEW POTATO KABOBS WITH GREEN CHILI SAUCE

Choose fresh broccoli that is a deep green color and has tightly closed buds. Broccoli stems are fully edible. This vegetable is high in vitamins and minerals.

8 Servings

Green Chili Sauce

- 2 cups plain non-fat yogurt
- 1 can, 4 ozs., chopped green, mild, or hot chilies, drained
- 1 tablespoon dried onion flakes
- ½ teaspoon each ingredient: ground cumin, garlic powder

- 8 double-pronged or bamboo skewers
- 16 new potatoes, skin on
- 2 cups broccoli florets
- 4 green onions, cut into 2-in. pieces
- 2 tablespoons lime juice, fresh-squeezed
- ½ teaspoon garlic powder
- ¼ teaspoon sage

Green Chili Sauce: Make sauce early in day. In a bowl, mix yogurt with drained chilies, onion flakes, cumin, and garlic powder. Cover lightly and refrigerate until ready to serve.

Scrub potatoes and cut into halves. Cook potatoes and broccoli, covered with water, until just cooked; cool. Thread skewers, alternating broccoli, potato halves, and onions, beginning and ending with broccoli.

In a cup, mix lime juice with garlic powder and sage. Brush vegetables with seasoned lime juice.

Preheat outdoor grill until coals are glowing. Spray grill and position kabobs 6 inches from heat source. Cook, turning and brushing, until vegetables begin to char. Kabobs are done when vegetables are hot and browned slightly.

To serve, place skewers on individual plates and drizzle with chili sauce.

Nutritional Data

PER SERVING		EXCHANGES	
Calories:	87	Milk:	0.0
Fat (gm):	0.3	Veg.:	0.5
Cholesterol (mg):	1	Fruit:	0.0
Sodium (mg):	52	Bread:	1.0
Potassium (mg):	449	Meat:	0.0
Sat. fat (gm):	0.1	Fat:	0.0
% Calories from fat:	3		

GRILLED POTATO SKINS WITH SALSA

♦

"Salsa" means sauce in Spanish, and what a sauce it is, usually a chopped-vegetable mixture with a blend of spices. You can adjust the spiciness by adding more or less hot pepper to taste. Reserve the meat of the potatoes for another dish.

♦

8 Servings

Salsa

- 4 medium tomatoes, peeled, coarsely chopped
- ¾ cup onions, chopped
- 1 large red bell pepper, seeded, chopped
- 3 cloves garlic, minced
- 2 jalapeño peppers, or to taste, seeded, chopped (use rubber gloves when preparing hot peppers)
- ½ cup cilantro, chopped
- ¼ teaspoon ground cumin, or cumin seeds
- 2 tablespoons lime juice, fresh-squeezed

Potato Skins

- 4 baking potatoes, about 6 ozs. each, skin on, scrubbed
  Non-stick cooking spray
- 2 tablespoons non-fat Italian salad dressing
- 1 teaspoon garlic powder
- 1 teaspoon cumin seeds

S alsa can be prepared the day before or early in the morning. Place tomatoes in mixing bowl. Toss tomatoes with onions, peppers, garlic, jalapeño peppers, cilantro, cumin, and lime juice. Taste to adjust seasonings. Cover and refrigerate until serving time. Toss salsa again before you serve it.

Potato Skins: Scrub potatoes under cold running water. Prick potatoes several times with tip of sharp knife. Bake on grill, wrapped in aluminum foil, or in preheated 425°F. oven about 1 hour or until done.

When potatoes are cool enough to handle, cut into halves horizontally. Scoop out insides, leaving ¼ inch of potato lining the skins. Reserve potato meat for another recipe. Cut potato skins again in half horizontally.

When coals are hot, position sprayed grill screen or rack on grill. Place potato skins, skin side down, on grill screen. Brush potatoes with Italian dressing as you turn them. Sprinkle with garlic powder and cumin seeds. Turn potato skins as necessary until they are hot and charred on both sides.

Using a long-handled spatula, remove potato skins to serving plate. Serve with salsa. Allow guests to either dip potato skins or spread a small amount of salsa onto each skin.

Nutritional Data

PER SERVING		EXCHANGES	
Calories:	87	Milk:	0.0
Fat (gm):	0.4	Veg.:	0.5
Cholesterol (mg):	0	Fruit:	0.0
Sodium (mg):	126	Bread:	1.0
Potassium (mg):	388	Meat:	0.0
Sat. fat (gm):	0	Fat:	0.0
% Calories from fat:	4		

New Potato, Artichoke, and Red Onion Kabobs

At the end of summer when the herbs have thick, woody stems, I harvest stems to use as skewers. Remove the herbs, trim stems, and make a point at one end using a small, sharp knife. These skewers add more flavor to kabobs and also make charming gifts.

8 Servings

8 rosemary skewers, double-pronged skewers, or bamboo skewers

2 large red onions, cut into halves, separated into leaves

16 new potatoes, skin on, parboiled until just fork tender, drained and sliced

8 marinated artichoke hearts
Non-stick cooking spray

Rosemary Brushing Sauce

1 tablespoon olive oil

¼ teaspoon rosemary

⅛ teaspoon garlic powder

1 tablespoon parsley, minced

T hread skewers, beginning with a leaf of onion, potato, onion, artichoke, onion, potato, onion. Add any extra onions at end of skewers.

Rosemary Brushing Sauce: Combine all sauce ingredients in small bowl. Brush kabobs with sauce.

Preheat outdoor grill until coals are glowing. Coat grill screen or rack with cooking spray and position it over hot coals, about 6 inches from heat source. Put kabobs on grill and cook, turning, as vegetables begin to char. Kabobs are done when vegetables are hot and browned slightly.

To serve, place skewers on individual plates and serve hot.

Nutritional Data

PER SERVING		EXCHANGES	
Calories:	145	Milk:	0.0
Fat (gm):	3.7	Veg.:	2.0
Cholesterol (mg):	0	Fruit:	0.0
Sodium (mg):	117	Bread:	1.0
Potassium (mg):	667	Meat:	0.0
Sat. fat (gm):	0.5	Fat:	0.5
% Calories from fat:	21		

GRILLED SWEET POTATOES WITH PINEAPPLE

Grilled Sweet Potatoes with Pineapple slices has a slight sweet-and-sour taste. It is good with both fish and chicken. Fresh ginger root should be stored in the refrigerator or in wine and then refrigerated.

8 Servings

- 4 sweet potatoes, 5–6 ozs. each, peeled
- 8 green onions, trimmed, leave whole
- 4 slices unsweetened pineapple, drained
- ¼ cup non-fat sweet-and-sour salad dressing
  Non-stick cooking spray
- 1 teaspoon ginger root, grated
- ½ teaspoon garlic powder
- ⅛ teaspoon cayenne pepper
- 1 tablespoon capers, drained

ook sweet potatoes in water until almost done. Drain. When potatoes are cool enough to handle, cut into ½-inch slices. Brush both potatoes and onions with sweet-and-sour salad dressing.

When coals are hot, set sprayed grill screen in place on grill. Position potato slices, green onions, and pineapple slices on screen. Sprinkle with ginger, garlic, and cayenne pepper.

Cook until food is just charred and hot. Turn frequently, as necessary. It might be necessary to brush food with salad dressing as it cooks or as you turn it.

Using long-handled spatula, remove food to serving bowl. Cut pineapple in half. Sprinkle with capers and serve hot.

Nutritional Data

PER SERVING		EXCHANGES	
Calories:	100	Milk:	0.0
Fat (gm):	0.5	Veg.:	0.0
Cholesterol (mg):	0	Fruit:	0.5
Sodium (mg):	43	Bread:	1.0
Potassium (mg):	171	Meat:	0.0
Sat. fat (gm):	0	Fat:	0.0
% Calories from fat:	4		

9.
SIDE DISHES

New Potatoes with Sun-Dried Tomatoes

Potato Masala with Spinach

Colcannon

Carrot and Potato Pudding

Classic Potato Pudding

German Potato Pudding

Potato Vegetable Puree

Mashed Red Potatoes with Onion Confit

Potato and Celery Seed Pie

Turkey Sausage Winnetka

Cuban Piped Mashed Potatoes

One Potato Pancake for 3 Guests

Sweet and White Potato Wedges

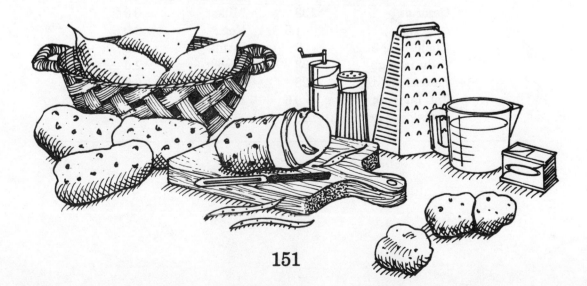

NEW POTATOES WITH SUN-DRIED TOMATOES

Try an easy and elegant way to herald in spring.

8 Servings

2 lbs. small red or new potatoes, skin on
  Olive oil, or non-stick cooking spray
1 tablespoon non-cholesterol margarine
⅓ cup reconstituted sun-dried tomatoes, chopped
½ cup parsley, minced
¼ teaspoon each ingredient: salt, pepper, chili powder
3 tablespoons Parmesan cheese, fresh-grated

Scrub potatoes and place on non-stick cookie sheet that has been sprayed or lightly coated with oil. Bake in preheated 400°F. oven 35 minutes or until potatoes are fork tender. Place potatoes in serving bowl.

Toss potatoes with margarine, tomatoes, parsley, salt, pepper, and chili powder. Sprinkle with Parmesan cheese. Serve hot.

Nutritional Data

PER SERVING		EXCHANGES	
Calories:	133	Milk:	0.0
Fat (gm):	1.6	Veg.:	0.0
Cholesterol (mg):	2	Fruit:	0.0
Sodium (mg):	138	Bread:	2.0
Potassium (mg):	528	Meat:	0.0
Sat. fat (gm):	0.6	Fat:	0.0
% Calories from fat:	10		

POTATO MASALA WITH SPINACH

A somewhat spicy but interesting dish. Good with many foods, such as chicken, meat, or fish. If you are a vegetarian, use it as a main dish.

6 Servings

    Olive oil, or non-stick cooking spray
- 1 tablespoon canola oil
- ¾ teaspoon ground cumin
- 4 cloves garlic, minced
- ½ teaspoon ginger root, fresh-grated
- 6 boiling potatoes, 5–6 ozs. each, skin on, diced
- 1 teaspoon curry powder
- ¼ teaspoon each ingredient: red chili flakes, salt, pepper, turmeric
- 12 ozs. fresh spinach, washed, trimmed
- 1 cup canned chickpeas, drained
- 1½ cups tomatoes, chopped
- ¼ cup cilantro, chopped

pray non-stick frying pan; or lightly coat with oil. Heat 1 tablespoon canola oil. Sprinkle pan with cumin, garlic, and ginger. Toss potatoes with spices, cover, and cook 4 to 6 minutes. Stir occasionally.

Stir in remaining ingredients, except cilantro. Cover and simmer 12 minutes or until potatoes are tender. Stir occasionally.

Spoon vegetables into serving bowl. Sprinkle with chopped cilantro. Serve hot.

Nutritional Data

PER SERVING		EXCHANGES	
Calories:	223	Milk:	0.0
Fat (gm):	3.6	Veg.:	1.0
Cholesterol (mg):	0	Fruit:	0.0
Sodium (mg):	320	Bread:	2.5
Potassium (mg):	1065	Meat:	0.0
Sat. fat (gm):	0.3	Fat:	0.5
% Calories from fat:	14		

COLCANNON

Colcannon can be found on restaurant menus from one end of the British Isles to the other. Translated in means "mashed potatoes cooked with thin slices of cabbage." An interesting vegetable combination.

8 Servings

2 cups plain cooked mashed potatoes, warm
4 cups green cabbage, finely shredded
1 carrot, sliced
1 turnip, chopped
  Canola oil, or non-stick cooking spray
2 tablespoons non-cholesterol margarine
4 green onions, trimmed, chopped
¼ teaspoon each ingredient: salt, pepper

Prepare all vegetables. Cook and mash potatoes. Cook cabbage, uncovered, in enough water to cover, 10 minutes or until tender, over medium-high heat. Drain. In separate pot, cover carrots and turnips with water and cook 10 minutes or until tender; drain and mash.

    Melt margarine in large non-stick frying pan that has been sprayed or lightly coated with oil. Cook onions until tender, covered. Add mashed potatoes, and vegetables. Stir together until hot. Season with salt and pepper. Spoon Colcannon into serving dish and serve hot.

Nutritional Data

PER SERVING		EXCHANGES	
Calories:	72	Milk:	0.0
Fat (gm):	1.9	Veg.:	0.0
Cholesterol (mg):	1	Fruit:	0.0
Sodium (mg):	279	Bread:	1.0
Potassium (mg):	329	Meat:	0.0
Sat. fat (gm):	0.4	Fat:	0.0
% Calories from fat:	21		

CARROT AND POTATO PUDDING

Potatoes meld well with many of the root vegetables. In this recipe we use carrots. This is a good fall dish when both potatoes and carrots are plentiful. It is the pine nuts that add a crunch to this pudding. You can sprinkle them on top or mix them into the pudding.

10 Servings

    Olive oil, or non-stick cooking spray
- 4 cups boiling potatoes, peeled, grated
- 4 large carrots, grated
- ¾ cup onions, grated
- 3 tablespoons non-cholesterol margarine
- 3 eggs, beaten
- 2 egg whites, stiffly beaten
- ½ cup plus 2 tablespoons fine cracker crumbs
- ¼ teaspoon each ingredient: salt, pepper, garlic powder
- 3 tablespoons pine nuts, toasted, optional

 Preheat oven to 350°F. Spray or lightly coat with oil a 2-quart ovenproof casserole or a 12-cup ring mold.

In large mixing bowl, blend potatoes, carrots, and onions. Mix in remaining ingredients.

Spoon pudding mixture into prepared casserole or ring mold. Bake in center of oven 55 to 60 minutes or until done. Pudding will be crusty on top. Serve hot.

Nutritional Data

PER SERVING		EXCHANGES	
Calories:	161	Milk:	0.0
Fat (gm):	6	Veg.:	1.0
Cholesterol (mg):	64	Fruit:	0.0
Sodium (mg):	173	Bread:	1.5
Potassium (mg):	395	Meat:	0.0
Sat. fat (gm):	0.8	Fat:	1.0
% Calories from fat:	28		

CLASSIC POTATO PUDDING

Potato puddings are known for the crust. Strange as it may seem, in our family we fight for more crust. It is crispy and tasty.

8 Servings

Non-stick cooking spray
3 egg whites, stiffly beaten
3 cups boiling potatoes, peeled, grated, well drained
1 egg, beaten
¼ cup potato flour or cornstarch
½ teaspoon baking powder
¼ teaspoon each ingredient: salt, pepper, garlic powder
½ cup onions, grated
1 tablespoon non-cholesterol margarine, melted

reheat oven to 375°F. Spray a 1½-quart casserole or other 6-cup ovenproof baking dish.

Beat egg whites until stiff but not dry. Mix in potatoes and remaining ingredients.

Spoon pudding mixture into prepared pan. Bake pudding 45 to 55 minutes or until crust is crispy and golden brown. Bring pudding to table hot and serve.

Nutritional Data

PER SERVING		EXCHANGES	
Calories:	100	Milk:	0.0
Fat (gm):	1.5	Veg.:	0.0
Cholesterol (mg):	27	Fruit:	0.0
Sodium (mg):	137	Bread:	1.5
Potassium (mg):	359	Meat:	0.0
Sat. fat (gm):	0.3	Fat:	0.0
% Calories from fat:	13		

GERMAN POTATO PUDDING

Potato pudding is just what the name implies, a pudding created from potatoes. Most potato puddings are German in origin. Usually a rather heavy dish, we have lightened it up a bit. It is a good dish for a buffet or just family fare.

8 Servings

1½ lbs. boiling potatoes, peeled, quartered
½ lb. parsnips, peeled, cut into 1-in. pieces
2 egg whites, lightly beaten
1 egg, lightly beaten
1 tablespoon non-cholesterol margarine
Canola oil, or non-stick cooking spray
½ cup onions, minced
¼ teaspoon each ingredient: salt, pepper, garlic powder
2 teaspoons cornstarch

Preheat oven to 375°F. Spray a 6-cup casserole.

To boil potatoes and parsnips together, cover with cold water in large saucepan. Bring to boil over high heat. Reduce to medium heat and continue cooking, uncovered, until potatoes are fork tender, about 20 minutes. Drain well; pat vegetables dry with paper towels.

Heat a non-stick frying pan and cook potatoes and parsnips 1 to 3 minutes, moving them vigorously as they cook by shaking the pan. This is to dry out the vegetables. Mash vegetables using potato masher, ricer with fine blade, or electric mixer. Blend in egg whites and egg.

Melt margarine in non-stick frying pan that has been sprayed or lightly coated with oil. Saute onions, partially covered, over medium heat until tender. Stir occasionally. Mix onions into vegetables. Flavor with salt, pepper, and garlic powder. Add cornstarch.

Spoon vegetables into prepared casserole and bake in center of oven 45 to 55 minutes. Top crust will be golden and crusty.

Nutritional Data

PER SERVING		EXCHANGES	
Calories:	123	Milk:	0.0
Fat (gm):	1.5	Veg.:	2.0
Cholesterol (mg):	27	Fruit:	0.0
Sodium (mg):	44	Bread:	1.0
Potassium (mg):	461	Meat:	0.0
Sat. fat (gm):	0.4	Fat:	0.0
% Calories from fat:	11		

POTATO VEGETABLE PUREE

This recipe is a tasty combination of pureed potatoes, turnips, and carrots seasoned with caraway seeds, thyme, and chives.

8 Servings

- 1 lb. boiling potatoes, peeled, cut into quarters
- ½ lb. turnips, peeled, cut into quarters
- 2 carrots, sliced
- 2–4 tablespoons low-salt Chicken Stock (see Index)
- 2 teaspoons non-cholesterol margarine
- 1 teaspoon caraway seeds
- ½ teaspoon thyme
- ¼ teaspoon each ingredient: salt, pepper
  Olive oil, or non-stick cooking spray
- ¼ cup chives or fresh parsley, chopped

T o boil potatoes, cover with 1 to 2 inches of cold water in large saucepan; bring to boil over high heat. Reduce to medium-high and cook, uncovered, until potatoes are fork tender, about 20 minutes; drain potatoes in colander. While still hot, mash potatoes using electric mixer, potato masher, or ricer. Potatoes should be free from lumps.

Cook and mash turnips and carrots together in the same way.

Combine potatoes, turnips, and carrots in bowl. Mix in stock, margarine, caraway seeds, thyme, salt, and pepper. Taste to adjust seasonings.

Spray or lightly coat with oil a non-stick saucepan. Heat the vegetable mixture, stirring as it heats. For an elegant effect, use a pastry bag with star tip and pipe the puree into individual portions or decorate a vegetable dish. Sprinkle with chopped chives.

Nutritional Data

PER SERVING		EXCHANGES	
Calories:	66	Milk:	0.0
Fat (gm):	0.6	Veg.:	1.0
Cholesterol (mg):	0	Fruit:	0.0
Sodium (mg):	99	Bread:	0.5
Potassium (mg):	313	Meat:	0.0
Sat. fat (gm):	0.1	Fat:	0.0
% Calories from fat:	81		

MASHED RED POTATOES WITH ONION CONFIT

My mother would fry onions until very brown and serve them mounded on top of buttery mashed potatoes. Long gone are the days of liberal use of butter, but perhaps this recipe will capture some of the flavor of that recipe.

8 Servings

1¾ lbs. red potatoes, scrubbed, peeled, cut into halves

2 teaspoons non-cholesterol margarine

⅓–½ cup skim milk

¼ teaspoon each ingredient: salt, pepper, ground nutmeg

Red Onion Confit

1 tablespoon non-cholesterol margarine

Olive oil, or non-stick cooking spray

2 cups red onions, thinly sliced

1 tablespoon dark brown sugar

1 tablespoon red wine vinegar

¼ teaspoon pepper

To boil potatoes, cover with cold water in large saucepan and bring to boil over high heat. Reduce heat to medium and continue cooking, uncovered, until potatoes are fork tender, about 20 minutes. Drain well and pat potatoes dry with paper towels.

Heat a non-stick frying pan and cook potatoes 1 to 2 minutes, moving potatoes vigorously as they cook by shaking the pan. This is to dry them out.

Mash potatoes using a potato masher, ricer with fine blade, or electric mixer. As you mash, blend in margarine, enough milk to make a smooth mashed potato, and seasonings.

Red Onion Confit: While potatoes are boiling, prepare onions. Melt margarine in a non-stick frying pan that has been sprayed or lightly coated with oil. Saute onions, partially covered, until tender, stirring occasionally. Mix in sugar, vinegar, and pepper as you cook.

To serve, mound potatoes in a vegetable dish or on individual plates. Make a depression in potatoes, using the back of a tablespoon. Spoon cooked onions onto potatoes. Serve hot.

Nutritional Data

PER SERVING		EXCHANGES	
Calories:	122	Milk:	0.0
Fat (gm):	1.4	Veg.:	1.0
Cholesterol (mg):	0	Fruit:	0.0
Sodium (mg):	104	Bread:	1.5
Potassium (mg):	463	Meat:	0.0
Sat. fat (gm):	0.3	Fat:	0.0
% Calories from fat:	10		

POTATO AND CELERY SEED PIE

This pie can be prepared in a rectangular pan as well as in a pie plate. It is good for a buffet, family dinner, or try it for lunch.

8 Servings

2¼ cups plain cooked mashed potatoes
¾ lb. low-fat small-curd cottage cheese
¼ cup plain non-fat yogurt
2 teaspoons non-cholesterol margarine
⅓ cup skim milk
1 egg, slightly beaten
1 teaspoon celery seeds
¼ teaspoon each ingredient: salt, white pepper, thyme, paprika
Olive oil, or non-stick cooking spray
2 teaspoons non-cholesterol margarine
1 cup green onions, chopped
2 cups celery, chopped

T o boil potatoes, cover with cold water in large saucepan and bring to boil over high heat. Reduce to medium heat and continue cooking, uncovered, until potatoes are fork tender, about 20 minutes. Drain and pat dry with paper towels. Cut into halves.

Heat non-stick frying pan and cook potatoes 1 to 2 minutes, moving them as they cook by shaking pan. This is to dry out potatoes.

Mash potatoes, using potato masher, ricer with fine blade, or electric mixer. Mix in cottage cheese and yogurt. While mashing potatoes, stir in margarine, milk, egg, and seasonings.

While potatoes are cooking, prepare onions and celery. Spray a non-stick frying pan or lightly coat with oil. Heat margarine. Saute onions and celery, covered, until tender, stirring occasionally. Mix into mashed potatoes.

Spray a 9-inch pie plate. Preheat oven to 400°F. Bake pie in center of oven about 30 minutes. Pie should be golden on top.

Nutritional Data

PER SERVING		EXCHANGES	
Calories:	109	Milk:	0.0
Fat (gm):	2.1	Veg.:	0.0
Cholesterol (mg):	30	Fruit:	0.0
Sodium (mg):	494	Bread:	1.0
Potassium (mg):	437	Meat:	0.5
Sat. fat (gm):	0.8	Fat:	0.0
% Calories from fat:	16		

TURKEY SAUSAGE WINNETKA

This recipe is from Sharon L. Gourley of Hess and Hunt, Winnetka, Illinois.

8 Servings

- 3 Italian-style turkey sausages, 5 ozs., cut into ½-in. pieces
- 2 large white onions, sliced
- 16 small red potatoes, skin on, quartered
- ¼ teaspoon each ingredient: salt, pepper, crushed red pepper flakes
- 2 large green bell peppers, seeded, cut into strips
- 1 can, 14½ ozs., Italian-style tomatoes, drained, chopped

Preheat oven to 375°F. Arrange sausage pieces, onions, and potatoes close together in single layer on non-stick cookie sheet. Sprinkle with salt, pepper, and pepper flakes. Bake 30 minutes.

Add green peppers to cookie sheet and continue baking until potatoes are tender and browned, 20 to 30 minutes. Stir in tomatoes last 5 to 10 minutes of baking.

Spoon into bowl and serve hot.

Nutritional Data

PER SERVING		EXCHANGES	
Calories:	114	Milk:	0.0
Fat (gm):	3.4	Veg.:	1.0
Cholesterol (mg):	14	Fruit:	0.0
Sodium (mg):	276	Bread:	1.0
Potassium (mg):	438	Meat:	0.5
Sat. fat (gm):	0.5	Fat:	0.0
% Calories from fat:	26		

CUBAN PIPED MASHED POTATOES

Take time to present mashed potatoes with style. Garlic, fennel seeds, and a dash of nutmeg are seasonings of choice for mashed potatoes. For extra flavor, add a few cloves of peeled, mashed garlic or bay leaves to the water when boiling potatoes. Mashed potatoes should be light and, of course, free from lumps.

8 Servings

- 2 lbs. boiling potatoes, peeled, quartered
- 3 cloves garlic, peeled
- 2 teaspoons non-cholesterol margarine
- ⅓–½ cup skim milk
- ½ teaspoon fennel seeds
- ¼ teaspoon white pepper
- ⅛ teaspoon ground nutmeg

Piped Potatoes
- 2 egg whites, slightly beaten
- Large pastry bag fitted with star tip
- Non-stick cooking spray

To boil potatoes and garlic, cover with cold water in large saucepan and bring to boil over high heat. Reduce to medium heat and continue cooking, uncovered, until potatoes are fork tender, about 20 minutes. Drain well; pat dry with paper towels.

Heat a non-stick frying pan and cook potatoes 1 to 2 minutes, moving potatoes vigorously as they cook by shaking pan. This is to dry out potatoes.

Mash potatoes using a potato masher, ricer with fine blade, or electric mixer. As you mash potatoes, blend in mashed garlic, margarine, and milk, using only as much milk as necessary to make smooth mashed potatoes. Season potatoes with fennel, white pepper, and nutmeg to taste. Serve potatoes warm, or make piped roses (see below).

Piped Potatoes: To make piped potato roses, mix 2 slightly beaten egg whites into potatoes. Spoon cooled potatoes into large pastry bag fitted with star tip. Pipe potatoes into rose-shaped mounds onto sprayed cookie sheet or onto edge of heatproof casserole or serving dish. Place potatoes under broiler, on middle rack, and cook only until potatoes begin to brown. Using a spatula, set potato roses on individual plates and serve.

Nutritional Data

PER SERVING		EXCHANGES	
Calories:	112	Milk:	0.0
Fat (gm):	0.6	Veg.:	0.0
Cholesterol (mg):	0	Fruit:	0.0
Sodium (mg):	35	Bread:	1.5
Potassium (mg):	465	Meat:	0.0
Sat. fat (gm):	0.1	Fat:	0.0
% Calories from fat:	5		

ONE POTATO PANCAKE FOR 3 GUESTS

The recipe doubles easily, so make as many pancakes as you need. Use the spatula to reshape pancake if necessary. Good with a dollop of plain non-fat yogurt and chopped green onions.

3 Servings

2 baking potatoes, 5–6 ozs. each, scrubbed, boiled
  Olive oil, or non-stick cooking spray
¼ teaspoon salt
¼ cup green onions, minced
2 cloves garlic, minced
1 tablespoon olive oil

 o boil potatoes, cover with cold water in large saucepan and bring to boil over high heat. Reduce to medium heat and continue cooking, uncovered, until potatoes are fork tender, about 20 minutes. Drain well; pat potatoes dry with paper towels. When potatoes are cool enough to handle, remove skins. Roughly grate potatoes.

Spray a 7-inch frying pan or lightly coat with oil. Heat and sprinkle salt, onions, and garlic on bottom of pan. Spread potatoes evenly over onions and garlic. Pat potatoes with spatula. Cook pancake over medium heat until crisp on bottom, 5 to 6 minutes.

Invert pancake onto plate, and with aid of spatula, slide it back into frying pan. Continue cooking another 5 to 6 minutes or until pancake is crisp on both sides. Using a spatula, remove pancake to serving dish. Serve hot.

Nutritional Data

PER SERVING		EXCHANGES	
Calories:	141	Milk:	0.0
Fat (gm):	4.6	Veg.:	0.0
Cholesterol (mg):	0	Fruit:	0.0
Sodium (mg):	183	Bread:	1.5
Potassium (mg):	431	Meat:	0.0
Sat. fat (gm):	0.7	Fat:	1.0
% Calories from fat:	29		

Sweet and White Potato Wedges

You can cook the recipe as it is written or use only sweet or only white potatoes. We think this is a good combination, however.

---

8 Servings

3 baking potatoes, 5–6 ozs. each, skin on, scrubbed, quartered horizontally

3 sweet potatoes, 5–6 ozs. each, skin on, scrubbed, quartered horizontally

Non-stick cooking spray

1 tablespoon olive oil

¾ teaspoon garlic powder

1 teaspoon caraway seeds

1 teaspoon thyme

reheat oven to 425°F. Arrange potatoes on sprayed, non-stick cookie sheet. Sprinkle potatoes with oil, garlic, caraway seeds, and thyme. Turn potatoes 3 or 4 times as they cook to brown on all sides. Bake potatoes 45 minutes or until fork tender.

Remove potatoes with spatula. Serve hot. You might want to have caraway seeds on the table for anyone who wants to add extra flavor.

Nutritional Data

PER SERVING		EXCHANGES	
Calories:	123	Milk:	0.0
Fat (gm):	1.8	Veg.:	0.0
Cholesterol (mg):	0	Fruit:	0.0
Sodium (mg):	8	Bread:	2.0
Potassium (mg):	413	Meat:	0.0
Sat. fat (gm):	0.3	Fat:	0.0
% Calories from fat:	13		

10.
Breads and Desserts

Sweet Potato Bread

Refrigerator Potato Rolls with Poppy Seeds

Sweet Potato Biscuits

Dill Potato Biscuits

Whole-Wheat Potato English Muffins

Potato Crumpets

Sweet Potato Pie

Bohemian Dessert Pancakes

Mashed Potato Waffles

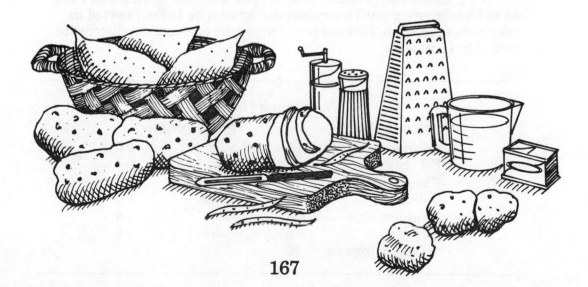

Sweet Potato Bread

Next day, toast thin slices of Sweet Potato Bread and serve warm.

10 Servings

1¾ cups all-purpose flour
1 teaspoon baking powder
1 teaspoon baking soda
¾ teaspoon ground cinnamon
¼ teaspoon ground nutmeg
⅛ teaspoon ground allspice
1 egg
½ cup lightly packed light brown sugar
4 tablespoons non-cholesterol margarine, room temperature
¾ cup cooked mashed sweet potatoes, room temperature
½–¾ cup skim milk
1 teaspoon vanilla

reheat oven to 350°F. Grease 5 × 9-inch loaf pan. Adjust rack to center of oven.

Sift flour, baking powder, baking soda, and spices together. Set aside.

Using large bowl of electric mixer, beat egg with brown sugar and margarine. Blend in mashed sweet potatoes, milk, and vanilla.

Pour batter into prepared pan. Set pan in center of oven and bake 45 to 55 minutes or until a bamboo skewer or cake tester inserted in cake comes out clean. Remove bread from pan; cool completely on wire rack. Slice and serve.

Nutritional Data

PER SERVING		EXCHANGES	
Calories:	180	Milk:	0.0
Fat (gm):	3.1	Veg.:	0.0
Cholesterol (mg):	21	Fruit:	0.0
Sodium (mg):	186	Bread:	2.5
Potassium (mg):	133	Meat:	0.0
Sat. fat (gm):	0.6	Fat:	0.0
% Calories from fat:	16		

REFRIGERATOR POTATO ROLLS WITH POPPY SEEDS

Once mashed potatoes are added to a batter, it becomes feathery light. The poppy seeds are an optional addition to these rolls. Do not grease the pan in which the dough rises.

16 Rolls (1 per serving)

½ cup skim milk
½ cup plain cooked mashed potatoes, warm
¼ cup non-cholesterol margarine, room temperature
2 tablespoons sugar
½ teaspoon salt
¼ cup warm water, between 105° and 115°F.
1 package active dry yeast
1 egg
2 egg whites
3 cups all-purpose flour, divided
1 teaspoon poppy seeds

In small saucepan, scald milk. Cool. Combine milk with mashed potatoes, margarine, sugar, and salt.

While mixture is cooling, pour water in measuring cup. Sprinkle yeast over water and stir to mix yeast with water. Set aside in warm area of kitchen for about 5 minutes. Yeast will begin to bubble. Stir yeast into potato mixture. Stir in egg, egg whites, and 1½ cups flour.

Place dough in deep bowl, cover with kitchen towel, and position in warm, draft-free area of kitchen. Dough will be loose. Allow to rise about 1 hour or until dough has doubled in bulk. Mix in remaining flour and poppy seeds. Return dough to bowl, cover, and refrigerate at least 2 hours.

Preheat oven to 400°F. Grease 2 muffin pans. Break off walnut-sized pieces of dough; knead each into a ball. Place dough balls in prepared pan. Transfer to dry area and allow to rise about 1 hour. Bake rolls about 15 minutes or until they test done. Rolls will be golden brown.

Nutritional Data

PER SERVING		EXCHANGES	
Calories:	120	Milk:	0.0
Fat (gm):	2.1	Veg.:	0.0
Cholesterol (mg):	13	Fruit:	0.0
Sodium (mg):	68	Bread:	1.5
Potassium (mg):	77	Meat:	0.0
Sat. fat (gm):	0.4	Fat:	0.5
% Calories from fat:	16		

SWEET POTATO BISCUITS

Add Southern flavor to your meal with these down-home biscuits.

14 Biscuits (1 per serving)

1 cup plain cooked mashed sweet potatoes
2 cups all-purpose flour
2 teaspoons baking powder
½ teaspoon baking soda
3 tablespoons light brown sugar
1 teaspoon ground cinnamon
¼ teaspoon ground cloves
½ cup dark raisins, optional
1 cup buttermilk
1½ tablespoons non-cholesterol margarine,
    melted, cooled

reheat oven to 400°F. Prepare mashed potatoes and set aside. This can be done early in day.

In large mixing bowl, combine flour, baking powder, baking soda, brown sugar, cinnamon, and cloves. Mix in raisins, buttermilk, margarine, and sweet potatoes. Batter will not be smooth.

Drop batter by heaping tablespoons onto non-stick cookie sheet. Bake biscuits 14 to 15 minutes or until light brown and firm on top. Biscuits are best served warm.

Nutritional Data

PER SERVING		EXCHANGES	
Calories:	113	Milk:	0.0
Fat (gm):	1	Veg.:	0.0
Cholesterol (mg):	1	Fruit:	0.0
Sodium (mg):	112	Bread:	1.5
Potassium (mg):	99	Meat:	0.0
Sat. fat (gm):	0.2	Fat:	0.0
% Calories from fat:	8		

DILL POTATO BISCUITS

These biscuits are easy to prepare. Change the herb to any one you prefer. Basil and rosemary are both good choices.

14 Biscuits (1 per serving)

1 cup plain cooked mashed potatoes, warm
2 cups all-purpose flour
2 teaspoons baking powder
½ teaspoon baking soda
3 tablespoons sugar
1 tablespoon fresh dill, chopped, or 1 teaspoon dill seeds
1 cup buttermilk
1½ tablespoons non-cholesterol margarine, melted, cooled

 Preheat oven to 400°F. Prepare mashed potatoes and set aside. This can be done early in day.

In large mixing bowl, combine flour, baking powder, baking soda, sugar, and dill. Mix in buttermilk, margarine, and potatoes.

Drop batter by heaping tablespoons onto non-stick cookie sheet. Bake biscuits 14 to 15 minutes or until light brown and firm on top. Biscuits are best served warm.

Nutritional Data

PER SERVING		EXCHANGES	
Calories:	99	Milk:	0.0
Fat (gm):	1.0	Veg.:	0.0
Cholesterol (mg):	1	Fruit:	0.0
Sodium (mg):	154	Bread:	1.5
Potassium (mg):	91	Meat:	0.0
Sat. fat (gm):	0.3	Fat:	0.0
% Calories from fat:	9		

WHOLE-WHEAT POTATO ENGLISH MUFFINS

It is the potatoes that give the English-style muffins their lightness. Use a 2¹/₂-inch or 3-inch crumpet ring, or, easier yet, cook muffins free form.

10 Muffins (1 per serving)

1 package active dry yeast
¼ cup warm water, between 105° and 110°F.
7 teaspoons instant mashed potatoes
1 cup hot water, divided
1¾ cups all-purpose flour
¾ cup whole-wheat flour
¼ teaspoon salt
2–3 tablespoons warm water
1 tablespoon non-cholesterol margarine

roof yeast. Pour warm water in measuring cup. Sprinkle yeast over water and stir to mix. Set aside in warm area of kitchen for about 5 minutes. Yeast will begin to bubble.

Meanwhile, dissolve potatoes in ½ cup hot water. Mix in remaining water.

Put flours and salt in mixing bowl. Mix in yeast and potatoes; using wooden spoon, stir for about 1 minute. Batter will be thick.

Cover bowl with clean kitchen towel or aluminum wrap and set in warm area of kitchen to rise. Bubbles will form on surface. Let rise until double in bulk, about 1 hour.

Stir batter down and mix in 2 to 3 tablespoons warm water, making a sticky dough. Again, cover dough and allow to rise until double in bulk and bubbles form on dough surface.

Melt margarine in non-stick frying pan. Drop batter to desired size (about 2 tablespoons), and cook on both sides until golden brown and cooked through. Serve warm, or split and toast.

Nutritional Data

PER SERVING		EXCHANGES	
Calories:	120	Milk:	0.0
Fat (gm):	1	Veg.:	0.0
Cholesterol (mg):	0	Fruit:	0.0
Sodium (mg):	76	Bread:	1.5
Potassium (mg):	83	Meat:	0.0
Sat. fat (gm):	0.2	Fat:	0.0
% Calories from fat:	7		

POTATO CRUMPETS

◆

Use potato Crumpets with natural jelly as a dessert or as a side dish with your entree.

◆

8 Crumpets (1 per serving)

2 cups plain cooked mashed potatoes, warm
1 egg white, slightly beaten
½ teaspoon thyme
¼ teaspoon white pepper
1 teaspoon non-cholesterol margarine, melted, cooled
⅓ cup all-purpose flour
¼ teaspoon baking soda
  Canola oil, or non-stick cooking spray
2 teaspoons non-cholesterol margarine

 Put mashed potatoes in mixing bowl. Beat in egg white, thyme, pepper, and melted margarine. Sift flour and baking powder over batter, using only enough flour to make a pliable dough.

Roll out dough on lightly floured pastry cloth. Cut out rounds, using 2 to 2½-inch cookie cutter.

Spray or oil a non-stick frying pan and melt 2 teaspoons margarine. Cook crumpets on hot surface about 3 minutes on each side or until golden brown. Serve hot.

◆

Nutritional Data

PER SERVING		EXCHANGES	
Calories:	68	Milk:	0.0
Fat (gm):	1.1	Veg.:	0.0
Cholesterol (mg):	1	Fruit:	0.0
Sodium (mg):	207	Bread:	1.0
Potassium (mg):	168	Meat:	0.0
Sat. fat (gm):	0.3	Fat:	0.0
% Calories from fat:	14		

◆

SWEET POTATO PIE

Sweet Potato Pie is the recipe that one automatically thinks about when considering a potato dessert. It is a very sweet and rich dessert. Our adaptation uses very little sweetener and a lot of spices. The crust is just a sprinkling of graham cracker crumbs instead of the traditional butter crust.

8 Servings

½ cup graham cracker crumbs
1½ cups cooked mashed sweet potatoes or yams
¼ cup egg substitute
2 egg whites, lightly beaten
¼ cup dark brown sugar
1 tablespoon candied ginger, chopped, optional
1 teaspoon ground cinnamon
½ teaspoon ground ginger
¼ teaspoon each ingredient: ground cloves, ground nutmeg, salt
1 cup buttermilk

reheat oven to 375°F. Adjust rack to center of oven. Sprinkle graham cracker crumbs over bottom of 9-inch pie plate.

Using a large bowl, combine sweet potatoes, eggs, brown sugar, candied ginger, spices, and buttermilk. Beat together all ingredients in large bowl of electric mixer until combined. Pour mixture into prepared pie plate.

Bake 50 to 55 minutes or until pie is done. Pie tests done when a bamboo skewer or other pie tester is inserted and comes out clean. Cool pie before serving. You can garnish pie with a dollop of non-fat dairy whip if desired.

Nutritional Data

PER SERVING		EXCHANGES	
Calories:	151	Milk:	0.0
Fat (gm):	2.2	Veg.:	0.0
Cholesterol (mg):	1	Fruit:	0.0
Sodium (mg):	176	Bread:	2.0
Potassium (mg):	221	Meat:	0.0
Sat. fat (gm):	0.3	Fat:	0.0
% Calories from fat:	13		

BOHEMIAN DESSERT PANCAKES

What a good use for leftover mashed potatoes. This recipe is great as a side dish or as a dessert.

8 Pancakes (1 per serving)

2 cups cooked mashed potatoes, cold
½ teaspoon ground cinnamon
¼ teaspoon each ingredient: ground nutmeg, salt
½ cup all-purpose flour
  Butter-flavored non-stick cooking spray
1 tablespoon non-cholesterol margarine
8 teaspoons low-calorie strawberry jam

 In mixing bowl, combine cold mashed potatoes, cinnamon, nutmeg, salt, and flour. You may want to knead dough to make sure all ingredients are well blended.

Divide dough into 8 equal pieces. Knead each piece into a ball; roll balls out on lightly floured surface. It is a good idea to use a cloth surface and a sleeve on rolling pin. Roll dough out thin.

Spray a well-seasoned frying pan. Melt margarine. Using spatula, transfer 1 pancake to pan; cook over medium heat until golden brown on bottom. Turn once with spatula and continue cooking until pancake is done on both sides. If bubbles form during cooking, pierce them with fork.

Spread each pancake with 1 teaspoon strawberry jam. Roll up pancake. Place it seam side down on dessert dish and serve hot. If you prepare pancakes before serving time, reheat them in 275°F. oven.

Nutritional Data

PER SERVING		EXCHANGES	
Calories:	77	Milk:	0.0
Fat (gm):	0.4	Veg.:	0.0
Cholesterol (mg):	1	Fruit:	0.0
Sodium (mg):	231	Bread:	1.0
Potassium (mg):	170	Meat:	0.0
Sat. fat (gm):	0.2	Fat:	0.0
% Calories from fat:	4		

MASHED POTATO WAFFLES

My husband says that these are a cross between a potato pancake and a waffle. With that comment in mind, let's serve the waffle with a dollop of yogurt. It is most important that the batter stands for 20 minutes before cooking.

4 Waffles (1 per serving)

¾ cup all-purpose flour
1 tablespoon sugar
1½ teaspoons baking powder
½ teaspoon baking soda
¼ teaspoon salt
2 egg whites
4 teaspoons non-cholesterol margarine, melted, cooled
1 cup buttermilk
1 cup plain cooked mashed potatoes
Canola oil, or non-stick cooking spray
¼ cup plain non-fat yogurt
¼ teaspoon ground cinnamon
⅛ teaspoon ground nutmeg

ift flour, sugar, baking powder, baking soda, and salt into a large bowl.

Lightly beat egg whites. Beat in cooled margarine and buttermilk. Add egg mixture to flour mixture. Add potatoes.

Heat sprayed or oiled waffle iron. Pour ¼ of waffle mixture into center of waffle iron. Cook until brown, according to individual manufacturer's directions.

In small bowl, combine yogurt, cinnamon, and nutmeg for topping.

Place waffles on individual plates and top each with tablespoon of cinnamon yogurt. Serve hot.

Nutritional Data

PER SERVING		EXCHANGES	
Calories:	189	Milk:	0.5
Fat (gm):	3	Veg.:	0.0
Cholesterol (mg):	3	Fruit:	0.0
Sodium (mg):	665	Bread:	2.0
Potassium (mg):	337	Meat:	0.0
Sat. fat (gm):	0.9	Fat:	0.0
% Calories from fat:	14		

Index

A

**APPETIZERS AND FIRST
  COURSE DISHES, 9–27**
Artichoke and Red Onion Kabobs,
  148
Asian Vegetables, Potatoes and, 49
Asparagus and Mushrooms over
  Baked Potatoes, 101

B

Baked Potato Party, 62
**BAKED POTATOES WITH
  TOPPINGS, 61–102**
Barley Potato Soup, 43
Bean Curd, Potatoes and, 52
Beet Soup with Potatoes and Yogurt, 40
Biscuits, Dill Potato, 172
Biscuits, Sweet Potato, 171
Black Bean Sauce, Steamed Potatoes
  in, 104
Bread, Sweet Potato, 168
**BREADS AND DESSERTS,
  167–178**
Broccoli and Potato Kabobs with
  Chili Sauce, 144
Buttermilk Soup, Summer Potato, 39

C

Catonese-Fried with Stuffed Peppers,
  14
Cantonese Stir-Fry Over Baked
  Potatoes, 89
Carrot and Potato Pudding, 155
Celery Seed and Potato Pie, 161
Chicken Fajitas Over Baked
  Potatoes, 99
Chicken, Moroccan, Over Baked
  Potatoes, 77

Chicken and Peanuts, Potatoes with,
  56
Chicken, Pea Pods, and Tomatoes,
  Potatoes with, 58
CHICKEN STOCK, 30
Chicken with Stone-Ground Mustard
  Over Baked Potatoes, 98
Chickpeas and Tomatoes Over Baked
  Potatoes, 87
Chili Sauce, New Potatoes with, 132
CHOWDER
  Maine Clam, 36
  New York City Clam, 34
  Potato-Fish, 37
Colcannon, 154
Couscous, Potatoes with, 46
Crab Cakes, Potato, 10
Crumpets, Potato, 175
Cuban Piped Mashed, 163
Cucumber-Potato Salad, 128
Curry Jacket Potatoes, 94
Curry Soup, 38

D

**DESSERTS AND BREADS,
  167–178**
Double-Baked Potatoes with Basil
  Sauce, 137
Dumplings, Russian Potato-Cheese, 26

E

Eggplant Parmesan Over Baked
  Potatoes, 69
English Muffins, Potato, 173

F

Fajitas, Vegetable, 85
Fish Chowder, 37
Fish-Potato Salad, 121

German Potato Salad, 122
Goulash Soup, 42
Green Bean and Walnut Potato
    Salad, 123
GRILLED POTATOES, 129–149

Hoisin Vegetables Over Baked
    Potatoes, 90
Indian-Flavored Vegetables Over
    Baked Potatoes, 68

Maine Clam Chowder, 36
Masala, Potato, with Spinach, 153
Mashed, Cuban Piped, 163
Mashed Potatoes with Onion Confit,
    159
Muffins, English, Potato, 173
Mushroom and Cheese Over Baked
    Potatoes, 93
Mushrooms, Two, Potatoes with, 51
Mussel-Potato Saffron Soup, 32

N

**NEW POTATOES, STEAMED,
    108, 114**
    in Black Bean Sauce, 104
    and Fennel with Wine, 112
    Oriental, 115
    and Tofu with Masala, 110
    with Yogurt and Olives, 106
New York City Clam Chowder, 34
Niçoise Salad Over Baked Potatoes,
    83

Orange Aroma, Steamed Potatoes
    with, 107
Oriental Steamed Potatoes, 115

Pancake for 3 Guests, 165
Pancakes, Bohemian Dessert, 177
Pancakes with Ginger Yogurt, 20
Pâté with Mushroom Sauce, 24
Peppers, Red, Potato-Stuffed, 12
Pie, Sweet Potato, 176
Pistou, 41
POTATOES
    History of, 2–4
    Nutrition in, 6–7
    Preparation of, 6
    Selection of, 5–6
    Storing, 6
    Varieties of, 4–5
**POTATOES ON THE GRILL,
    129–149**
POTATO SALADS, 117–128
    à la Caesar, 118
    Country with Mustard Dressing,
        120
    German, 122
    Green Bean and Walnut, 123
    Potato-Cucumber, 128
    Potato-Fish, 121
    Smoked Turkey, 125
    South American, 124
    Sweet, Grilled, 126
    Thai with Chicken, 119
Provençal Vegetables, Baked
    Potatoes with, 81
Pudding, Potato, 156, 157

R

Ratatouille, Potato, 76
Red Onions, Grilled with, 143
Rolls, Potato, with Poppy Seeds, 169

S

Salads, Potato, *see Potato Salads*
Salmon, Capers, and Dill, Potatoes
    with, 59
Salsa-Stuffed New Potatoes, 11
SIDE DISHES, 151–166
Shrimp and Asparagus Over Baked
    Potatoes, 64
Shrimp, Thai, Over Baked Potatoes, 71

Skins with Salsa, Grilled, 146
SOUP, 29–43
South American Potato Salad, 124
Spanakopita Baked Potatoes, 92
Spinach Balls, 15
STEAMED POTATOES,
103–115
STIR-FRY POTATOES,
45–60
STOCK
Chicken, 30
Vegetable, 31
Sun-Dried Tomatoes, New Potatoes
with, 152
SWEET POTATOES
Baked with Mandarin Oranges
and Cheese Topping, 74
with Peppers and Tomatoes, 140
with Pineapple, Grilled, 149
Steamed with Honey, 109
Stir-Fry with Beef and Water
Chestnuts, 47
Wedges, with White Potatoes, 166
Sweet Potato Biscuits, 171
Sweet Potato Bread, 168
Sweet Potato Pie, 176
Sweet Potato Salad, Grilled, 126

Tandoori Chicken and Potato
Kabobs, 136
Tandoori-Flavored Vegetable Kabobs,
134
Teriyaki with Pea Pods and
Mushrooms, 139
Thai Potato and Chicken Salad, 119
Tofu with Masala, Steamed Potatoes
and, 110
Tofu Veracruzana Over Baked
Potatoes, 66

Tomato and Melted Cheese Over
Baked Potatoes, 73
Turkey Chili Over Baked Potatoes,
79
Turkey Sausage Winnetka, 162
Turkey, Smoked, Potato Salad, 125

Vegetable Chili Over Baked
Potatoes, 96
Vegetable Fajitas, 85
Vegetable Potato Kabobs, 16
Vegetable, Potato, Puree, 158
Vegtable Stir-Fry with Mustard
Vinaigrette, 54
VEGETABLE STOCK, 31
Vegetables and Pasta, Grilled, 141
Vichyssoise, 33

Waffles, Mashed Potato, 178
Wedges, Potato, with Italian Tuna
Sauce, 18

Yogurt and Olives, New Potatoes
with, 106

Zucchini-Potato Pancakes with
Indian Sauce, 22